THE TESTAMENTS OF THE TWELVE PATRIARCHS
A CRITICAL HISTORY OF RESEARCH

by

H. Dixon Slingerland

Published by
SCHOLARS PRESS
for
The Society of Biblical Literature

Distributed by

SCHOLARS PRESS
University of Montana
Missoula, Montana 59812

THE TESTAMENTS OF THE TWELVE PATRIARCHS

A CRITICAL HISTORY OF RESEARCH

by

H. Dixon Slingerland

Library of Congress Cataloging in Publication Data
Slingerland, H. Dixon
　The Testaments of the twelve patriarchs.

　(Monograph series - Society of Biblical Literature ; no. 21)
　A revision of the author's thesis, Union Theological Seminary, 1973.
　Bibliography: p. 116

　1. Bible. O. T. Apocryphal books. Testaments
of the twelve patriarchs—Criticism, interpretation,
etc.—History. I. Title. II. Series: Society
of Biblical Literature. Monograph series ; no. 21.
BS1830.T5S57 1975　　229'.914　　75-34233
ISBN 0-89130-062-7

Printed in the United States of America

Edwards Brothers, Inc.
Ann Arbor, Michigan 48104

THE TESTAMENTS OF THE TWELVE PATRIARCHS
A CRITICAL HISTORY OF RESEARCH

SOCIETY OF BIBLICAL LITERATURE
MONOGRAPH SERIES

edited by
Leander Keck
Associate Editor
James L. Crenshaw

Number 21

THE TESTAMENTS OF THE TWELVE PATRIARCHS

A CRITICAL HISTORY OF RESEARCH

by
H. Dixon Slingerland

SCHOLARS PRESS
Missoula, Montana

To Bonnie

Preface

This study is the revision of a doctoral dissertation completed for Union Theological Seminary (New York) in 1973. Original impetus for the work was provided by a 1970 seminar on Jewish Christianity conducted by the New Testament faculty at Union Theological Seminary.

Many people deserve thanks for their help with this project. Professor Reginald H. Fuller, my major advisor, was constantly available as scholar and counselor. Professor J. Louis Martyn, Professor Raymond E. Brown, and Dean Cyril C. Richardson, the other members of the dissertation committee, were likewise generous with their time and assistance. Professor M. de Jonge provided much bibliographical material in his correspondence with me, and was gracious as my host in Leiden. Professor Martin Hengel met with me on several occasions to discuss the Testaments during my year as a student in Tübingen.

To Professor Leander E. Keck, Editor of the Society of Biblical Literature Monograph Series, I express much thanks for his penetrating observations and suggestions. His help contributed extensively to the last chapter of the present study. And finally, I feel a special debt of gratitude to Professor Arthur Vööbus, my seminary teacher of three years, who first revealed to me the rich and complex world of early Christian faith and life.

I wish to thank also the library staff of Union Theological Seminary. Without its patient hard work on my behalf, this study would not have been possible. Mr. Richard Spoor, the Reference Librarian at Union, deserves credit for procuring hard-to-find materials both in the United States and Europe. A number of other libraries are to be thanked as well: these include the libraries of Harvard Divinity School and Princeton Theological Seminary, the Universitätsbibliothek of Tübingen, and the Universitäts- und Landesbibliothek of Halle.

H. Dixon Slingerland
New York City
July 22, 1975

Table of Contents

CHAPTER I

Introduction

There is no document in the Pseudepigrapha more valuable than the Testaments of the Twelve Patriarchs. Where Qumran and its theology are discussed, so is the Testaments. Where the ethical teachings of Jesus are analyzed, the parallels in the Testaments must be considered. Where the eschatology and messianism of late Judaism and early Christianity are an issue, the same themes in the Testaments cannot be avoided. The Testaments contains remnants of ancient sources otherwise lost; it may be unique outside the New Testament in its double love-command and universal salvation. The doctrine of the two Messiahs claimed for it is paralleled only in the Qumran literature.

However, if the Testaments is among the most valuable writings in the Pseudepigrapha, it is also one of the most contested in terms of origin. Already by 1800 three theories had been presented on this issue. Some scholars said the Testaments was a Jewish document with Christian interpolations, valuable therefore as a primary source for intertestamental Judaism. Others said it was a Christian document, but disagreed among themselves whether it was a product of Gentile or Jewish Christianity. Yet even now the same disputes continue, and we can speak no more today than 175 years ago of the "sure results of scholarship" concerning Testaments origins. On the contrary, the theories of origins have multiplied in number. We can no longer ask, "Is the Testaments a Jewish document?" We must ask rather, "If the Testaments is a Jewish document, did it originate in the pre-Hasmonean, Hasmonean, or post-Hasmonean period? Is it the product of Qumran, or of the Pharisees, or of the Jewish Diaspora?" Nor can we ask, "Is it a Christian document?" We must ask rather, "Was it compiled, redacted, or only interpolated by Christian hands?"

This inability of scholarship to grapple successfully with the key question of the origin of the Testaments seriously diminishes the potential value of the document. With wide disagreement surrounding the community of its origin, only the bravest among scholars would dare use it as a primary source for the way of life and teachings of some ancient Jewish or Christian community.

Thus, for example, H. F. D. Sparks[1] has implied that the Testaments is of little value either in the study of Judaism or Christianity because of the uncertainty surrounding it. Moreover, during much of the 1960s discussion of the Testaments appeared primarily in the analyses of various theological themes, while the issue of origins was generally avoided.

Such a situation in the present state of scholarship is to be lamented, because the real value of the Testaments is its use as a primary source for the way of life of some ancient community(ies). Whether as a document in its original form, or as the redacted or interpolated version of some earlier document, it is after all the product of a particular time and place (or of times and places) and so provides us with that most exciting artifact, the literary photograph of an ancient Jewish or Christian community or communities. Unfortunately, however, this rich and detailed photograph has no inscription on the back telling us when and where it was taken; thus, just as with any such picture in the curio shop, each is left to try to make the identification in accord with what seems most familiar to him.

This is not to say that there have been no gains in the question of origins. Much work has been done on the Testaments during the past three centuries. Its similarities to and differences from the Dead Sea Scrolls have been carefully researched, as have its parallels in other Jewish and Christian literature. Theme studies abound, as do source- and literary-critical analyses; modern textual criticism has made tremendous steps in securing a dependable text of the Testaments. Regardless of these advances, however, we appear now perhaps more than ever to be at a roadblock concerning the most pressing question of the origins of this document. By 1860 there was no doubt that the Testaments represented the work of Christian hands, and it remained only to see if these were Gentile-Christian or belonged to a Nazarene or Ebionite Jewish Christian. In 1884 the consensus had been reached that the Testaments was a Nazarene-Christian document written before 135 C.E. Again, by 1908 there was a new consensus, as firm as the last, that the Testaments arose in Palestinian Judaism and had been interpolated by Christian hands. This consensus was finally shaken, however, in the early 1950s by both the Qumran discoveries and M. de Jonge's thesis of Christian compilation.

Unlike earlier decades, therefore, today it is no longer possible to speak of scholarship's consensus concerning Testaments origins. Extensive critical studies have left us with a breakdown in the consensus, and more important, with the awareness that scholarship's past presuppositions and methods have brought us farther from rather than closer to a resolution of the question of origins.

Such a situation is not all bad, however. It is wholesome in making clear to us that there is a serious problem of method. Therefore, the present study assumes the inconclusive outcome of the search for the origin of the Testaments. Specifically, this study presupposes that what is *not* needed most right now is another critical analysis done along previous lines. Rather, in the view of the present writer, the time is right to step back from the indecisive front-line critical battles, in order to gain a fresh view of the field and of the strategies which have appeared upon it. That is, the time has come to tally up exactly where we stand vis-à-vis the question of origins, to describe as precisely as possible the contours of the research landscape, and to show why the same critical methods have produced such contrasting results.

Therefore, the present study has two objectives. The first of these is a comprehensive history of research on the Testaments, found in Chapters 2 through 6. Besides existing for its own purpose, this history serves also as the rationale and justification for the second objective, the clarification and criticism of the presuppositions and methods which have so far guided Testaments research. Chapter 7 is directed toward this second objective.

It is appropriate to comment on these objectives. To begin with, the history itself is presented in a strictly chronological rather than topical order, in order to show as clearly as possible the various stages through which research has moved. This chronological approach will indicate the complex nature of these stages, thus avoiding the danger of harmonization or simplification. To assist the reader in comprehending this account, relationships and contours have been made clear wherever they exist; the writer has sought throughout to make as manageable as is honestly possible an otherwise highly complex and variegated history of research.

This history is significant in several ways. First, such a comprehensive work does not at present exist. The briefer histories of research written in the past century do not fill the need of a modern account. Although J. Becker's[2] recent book does contain a history, this is not complete since it omits all research (with the exception of Grabe) prior to 1884 and emphasizes the literary-critical analyses with which Becker's own work is closely associated. Second, the present history reveals where real gains have been made in scholarship. Thus, for example, it shows the multiplicity of literary-critical results but the near consensus in textual criticism. Third, it brings out of oblivion the important studies of such nineteenth century scholars as Nitzsch, Dorner, Ritschl, Kayser, Hilgenfeld, and Sinker. Because these men represent a now forgotten school of thought concerning the origins of the Testaments, it is both proper and important at the present moment to let their voices be heard again. Fourth, the history shows us the futility of trying to analyze any theme or form within the Testaments on the assumption of either the Jewish or Christian origin of the Testaments — common though such a procedure has been. Fifth, in clarifying the origins dilemma, the history of research exposes the need to clarify the relationship between the presuppositions and methods of scholarship. That is, it makes necessary the second objective, viz., the analysis of the presuppositions and methods of scholarship in its attempt to resolve the origins problem.

Whereas the history of research is descriptive, the approach to the second objective is analytical and critical. It seeks to clarify the presuppositions behind Jewish and Christian origins theories and to analyze the critical methods applied to the Testaments on the basis of these presuppositions.

Having done this, it proposes a slightly different set of presuppositions, which are commensurate with both the basic data of Testaments research and the results of our analysis of critical methods. Then, on the basis of these new presuppositions, a more inclusive approach is suggested for the resolution of the dilemma of origins.

FOOTNOTES

[1]H. F. D. Sparks, rev. of M. de Jonge, *The Testaments of the Twelve Patriarchs, JTS*, n.s. 6 (1955) 289.

[2]J. Becker, *Untersuchungen zur Entstehungsgeschichte der Testamente der zwölf Patriarchen* (Leiden: E. J. Brill, 1970).

CHAPTER II

The Testaments of the Twelve Patriarchs from the Beginning of Research until 1884

According to J. Becker's[1] description of the history of research on the Testaments of the Twelve Patriarchs, serious scholarly study of the Testaments began only with the work of F. Schnapp in 1884. Unfortunately, such a view prevails in nearly all present scholarship. When J. E. Grabe is mentioned it is not principally because of his scholarly introduction to the Testaments, but because in 1698 he offered the first printed edition of the Greek text.[2] Grabe's edition, however, has had a very important bearing on modern study of the origins of the Testaments. As noted above, Becker begins his history of research with F. Schnapp. But he does make the exception of mentioning one central part of Grabe's work, i.e., the view that the Testaments was a Jewish document later interpolated by Christian hands. In this way Becker establishes a bridge between these two men who held similar positions concerning the origins of the Testaments; and in this way also Becker affirms the popular view that the Testaments has always been judged to be a basically Jewish document.

F. Schnapp[3] made it clear that his position was a new one; he indicated that before him only Grabe had argued for the Jewish origin of the Testaments and that the consensus previous to his own work viewed the Testaments as a Christian writing. R. H. Charles, although he adopted the Grabe-Schnapp thesis, also described those earlier scholars who had argued for Christian origins.[4] But, as we shall see in Chapter 3, the work of Charles (and before him of Schnapp, Conybeare, Bousset, and Preuschen) won the day so completely in favor of Jewish origins that in this century almost no mention has been made of the many scholars before Schnapp who held a different position. Even those who now argue that the Testaments is a Christian document pay little attention to pre-Schnapp scholarship. Consequently, the argument that the Testaments is a Christian writing appears to be novel. It is as if M. de Jonge had been the first scholar, as late as 1953, to propose that the Testaments was a product of early Christianity.

5

The present chapter makes up for this serious past omission by tracing the history of research from the beginning of scholarly discussion of the Testaments to the year in which Schnapp offered his monograph (1884). The material may be organized into two sections. The first will deal with the Testaments in the earliest period of discussion, 1242 through 1781, in which a first resolution of the origins question was reached. The second will deal with the Testaments in the period from 1810 through 1883, in which the question of the Gentile- or Jewish-Christian origin of the Testaments was temporarily resolved.

1242 through 1781: Is the Testaments
a Jewish or a Christian Document?

Matthew Paris,[5] writing sometime shortly after the middle of the thirteenth century, described how Robert Grosseteste, Bishop of Lincoln, translated the Testaments from Greek into Latin in the year 1242. Beyond this, Paris notes that the Testaments had been hidden previously by the Jews *propter prophetias de salvatore in eis contentas*, but that the Greeks had discovered and faithfully translated it from Hebrew into their own language. Paris evidently believed that the Testaments was a Jewish document of value to the Church because of its prophetic allusions to the Messiah. Where Grosseteste acquired the Testaments is not clear.

On the last page of what may be the first printed edition of the Latin Version, possibly published ca. 1515, there is a similar tradition to that of Paris concerning the Testaments.[6] Here the unknown editor refers to the work of Bishop Robert and then repeats Paris' explanation for the late appearance of the Testaments, i.e., the Jews had hidden it. Again, in a German translation[7] of the Latin printed in 1544 but claiming to go back to a German text of 1431, the editors repeat all of the traditions handed down by Paris, including the view that the Greek is a translation of the Hebrew. In addition, they appear to offer an apology for their edition by writing that, while the legalism of the Testaments is unacceptable, its messianism is quite valuable and justifies the edition. Thus, by 1544 we find two explanations for the late publication of the Testaments: (1) the Jews had hidden it so as to conceal the messianic prophecies; (2) the Christians avoided it because of its Jewish teachings. Both of these explanations are based on the same assumption: the Testaments is a Jewish document written in Hebrew.[8]

This assumption brings us to J. E. Grabe, the editor of the *editio princeps* of the Greek text of the Testaments and the first scholarly defender of the view that the Testaments was indeed of Jewish origin and written in Hebrew.

Grabe's primary interests in his fifteen page introduction[9] are the question of the Jewish or Christian authorship and the century in which the Testaments was written. Concerning authorship, Grabe argues that a Christian writer would not describe the Messiah in the terms which appear in the Testaments, where he is pictured as bellicose and dying in war.[10] Again, seeing that the

Testaments uses much Jewish tradition and appears in many ancient lists as a part of the Old Testament Apocrypha,[11] Grabe concludes that the author must have been a Jew. However, given such clearly Christian passages as T Levi 18, he further concludes that the Testaments was written by a Jew, but later interpolated by Christian hands (*a christiano*).[12] As to the date of writing, he argues that the Jewish document is pre-Christian because 1) Paul used it in I Thes 2:16, and 2) the apocryphal literature classified with the Testaments in the ancient lists is pre-Christian.[13] Concerning the date of the Christian material, he concludes that T Levi 16 (on the destruction of the Temple) is Christian and post-70 C.E., probably added about 100 C.E.[14] In the final section, Grabe states that the Testaments was written originally in Hebrew. He bases this view on the report of M. Paris and on a colophon to an MS 75 which attributes the Greek text to a translation by John Chrysostom.[15]

However, shortly after the publication of Grabe's work, with its substantiation of the opinion of previous centuries that the Testaments is Jewish in origin,[16] two other discussions appeared which asserted that it was written originally in Greek and by a Christian. D. Le Nourry[17] (writing ca. 1700) agreed with Grabe that the Testaments was in existence before Origen. Because of the abundance of Christian material in the Testaments, however, Le Nourry concluded that it was the work of someone within the Church. Likewise, J. A. Fabricius,[18] arguing from the Greek style of the Testaments, dated it with the Shepherd of Hermas and Sibylline Oracles.

It was not until a half-century later[19] that A. Gallandi in 1765 next took up the subject of the Testaments. He affirmed the position of Fabricius that the Testaments was of Christian origin, written after the fall of the Temple but before Origen.[20]

So far, however, no one had refuted Grabe's major argument against the Christian origin of the Testaments, i.e., a Christian would not have written of the Messiah in war-like terms. Initial establishment of the theory of Christian origins may thus be credited to the man who refuted this argument, H. Corrodi. He disputes Grabe on two grounds.[21] First, granted that the Testaments does contain much Jewish and Christian material, Corrodi argues that the writer must have been a Jewish Christian, probably of the second century. Second, the writer could have used the tradition of a war-like Messiah because it appeared already in the Book of Revelation.

The scene is now set for all subsequent work on the Testaments. Between 1242 and 1781 relatively little had been written about the Testaments and that which had been written is superficial in comparison with later, far more detailed studies. Nonetheless, by 1781, the theses which would vie for acceptance in the modern discussion had all been set out. Grabe argued that the Testaments was a Jewish document written in Hebrew and later interpolated by a Christian. Le Nourry, Fabricius, and Gallandi saw a Christian document written originally in Greek; Corrodi a specifically Jewish-Christian writing.

1810 through 1883: Is the Testaments a Jewish-Christian
or a Gentile-Christian Document?

By 1781 the opinion had been expressed that the Testaments of the Twelve Patriarchs was a Christian writing. Nothing further was said on our subject, however, until some thirty years later when, in 1810, C. I. Nitzsch wrote the first introduction devoted solely to the Testaments. Nitzsch begins his short book with a general discussion of the Pseudepigrapha of the Old Testament, showing that in this body of literature there are Christian, Christian interpolated, and Jewish-Christian writings.[22] Within this last group he includes IV Esdras, the Psalms of Solomon, and the Testaments of the Twelve Patriarchs.[23]

Nitzsch then goes on to consider the Testaments specifically. He first deals with Grabe's theory that it is a Jewish document originally written in Hebrew. The original language, however, is Greek and not Hebrew according to Nitzsch, because the Testaments uses both paronomasia ($\dot{\alpha}\theta\epsilon\tau\epsilon\hat{\iota}\nu$ $\nu o\nu\theta\epsilon\tau\epsilon\hat{\iota}\nu$, $\dot{\alpha}\phi\alpha\acute{\iota}\rho\epsilon\sigma\iota\varsigma$, $\dot{\alpha}\nu\alpha\acute{\iota}\rho\epsilon\sigma\iota\varsigma$) and various Greek philosophical terms ($\delta\iota\acute{\alpha}\theta\epsilon\sigma\iota\varsigma$, $\alpha\check{\iota}\sigma\theta\eta\sigma\iota\varsigma$, $\phi\acute{\upsilon}\sigma\iota\varsigma$, $\tau\acute{\epsilon}\lambda o\varsigma$); these elements are not explicable on the theory of a Hebrew original.[24] Again, the Testaments is Christian because of the messianic description in T Levi 18 and the many other Christian elements in the document.[25]

Next Nitzsch concerns himself with the question of date. As clues to the terminus post quem he notes the reference to the fall of the Temple in 70 C.E. (T Levi 16:4), and the use of the New Testament. He concludes, therefore, that the terminus post quem must be ca. 100 C.E. The terminus ad quem is provided by the references in Tertullian and Origen. In the opinion of Nitzsch, therefore, the Testaments was written either at the beginning or in the middle of the second century.[26]

Finally, Nitzsch considers the question of where the Testaments was written. The supremacy of priesthood over kingship paralleled in Philo of Alexandria, the vocabulary similar to that of the Therapeutae, the asceticism like that of the Essenes, the allegory, and the eclectic philosophy of the Testaments all point to Alexandria in Nitzsch's view.[27]

For him, then, the Testaments was the product of an Alexandrian Jewish Christianity of the second century which took many of its major characteristics from the Jewish sects. Nitzsch's study seems, however, to have appeared in a vacuum. As noted above, nothing had been written on the Testaments in the thirty years prior to 1810. It will now be another thirty years before the topic of the Testaments is taken up again.

In 1845 I. A. Dorner concurs with Nitzsch that the writer of the Testaments was a Jewish Christian. For Dorner this is clear because T Jos 19:8 connects Mary closely to the Temple by reference to the linen garment. This in turn connects Jesus to the priesthood, establishing a relationship of interest only to Jewish Christians.[28] Again, Dorner dates the Testaments with Nitzsch in the second century (ca. 150 C.E.). His reasons, however, are the similarities of the Testaments to Barnabas and Aristo of Pella.[29] He does not say where it was written.

A most interesting section of Dorner's discussion is the composite picture of the "person and work" of Jesus which he draws from the Testaments. The following quotation from the English translation will make clear why for him the Testaments is a Christian document:

> The salvation of God ($\sigma\omega\tau\acute{\eta}\rho\iota o\nu$ $\tau o\hat{\upsilon}$ $\theta\epsilon o\hat{\upsilon}$) will arise on you in Him who is God and man (Sim. 7; Dan. 5; Benj. 9). The Lord, the great God of Israel, appears on earth as a man, assumes a body (Sim. 6); God visits ($\acute{\epsilon}\pi\iota\sigma\kappa\acute{\epsilon}\pi\tau\epsilon\tau\alpha\iota$) all peoples through the compassion of His Son (Levi 4); dwells among men amidst Israel (Levi 4,2; Naphth. 8), and eats with them (Sim. 6; Asshur 7). . . . Through His appearance is the visit of the Only-begotten ($\mu o\nu o\gamma\epsilon\nu\acute{\eta}s$), yet is He to appear on earth as a man of humiliation (Benj. 9,10). But in his humiliation He is nevertheless God come in the Flesh (Benj. 10) on account of whose birth men and angels, and the whole earth, rejoice. He is the Savior of the world (Levi 10,4). His baptism points to His sacrifice. The heavens are opened above Him.. . . [30]

Dorner continues in a similar manner with regard to Jesus' death and resurrection, and the final judgment as they are portrayed in our document.

Dorner's opinion that the Testaments was a Jewish-Christian writing caused an immediate upsurge in literature on the Testaments. A. Ritschl may have known of Nitzsch, but it was with Dorner in mind that he discussed the Testaments in 1850. Specifically, Ritschl[31] insists that this document is not Jewish-Christian, but Gentile-Christian in origin. Not only does the Law in the Testaments stress ethics instead of cult, but also Abraham (through his progeny) is emphasized instead of Moses, as in Paul; moreover, Paul himself is spoken of approvingly in T Benj 11:1.

For three decades before Dorner nothing had been written on the Testaments. Now, however, only one year after the appearance of Ritschl's discussion, A. Kayser published his very significant article.[32] Like Grabe, Kayser argues that within the Testaments two different hands are to be detected; but, unlike Grabe who said they were Jewish and Christian, Kayser sees them as Jewish-Christian and Gentile-Christian. He therefore applies literary criticism in order to resolve the dispute between Nitzsch-Dorner and Ritschl.

According to Kayser, the contradictory conclusions of Grabe, Nitzsch, and Ritschl suggest that the Testaments is not a literary unit.[33] But, since its purpose is to speak to the Jews concerning ethics and the Christian messianic future, the document is Christian. It comes either from a Gentile-(Pauline) or Jewish-Christian milieu.[34] To establish which of these alternatives is correct, Kayser then suggests that various theological criteria should be applied to the Testaments.

The first criterion is its strong nationalism:

> In jenen Erzählungen und dieser Weissagung [T Judah 11, 16, 19] äussert sich ein Interesse an dem semitischen Geschlecht dem kanaanitischen, hamitischen gegenüber, wie dasselbe nur bei einem gebornen Juden oder Judenchristen denkbar, dem Paulus durchaus fremd ist.[35]

Because the only parallel to the Ham/Shem materials appears in the Kerygma Petri (Clementine Recognitions I.30, 32, 33), an Ebionite document, the Testaments also must be the product of Ebionite Jewish Christianity.[36]

The second criterion is the two-fold christology of the Testaments[37] in which Jesus is both a man set aside by the Holy Spirit at baptism (T Naph 4; T Levi 16, 18; T Judah 24) and also God (T Levi 2; T Sim 6; T Asher 7). Since the former view is Ebionite and the latter patripassionistic, Kayser concludes that one of the two must be an interpolation. But which?

T Sim 6 provides the first clue in answer to this question. T Sim 6:4,5 is modalistic, patripassionistic. But it is also an interpolation. First, verse 4 is contradictory, offering both the destruction of Ham yet also universal salvation; second, the use of the present participle $\phi\alpha\iota\nu\acute{o}\mu\epsilon\nu os$ rather than the future indicative is awkward; third, one of Grabe's MSS omits "as man"; fourth, the Latin implies $\acute{o}\tau\epsilon$ for $\acute{o}\tau\iota$; fifth, the God-man conception breaks in crudely.[38]

A second clue is given by T Levi 4 where the patripassionistic section (T Levi 4:1) breaks into an otherwise homogeneous context.[39] From this evidence Kayser concludes that the original text of the Testaments did not contain the Gentile-Christian partripassionism, but was the product of an Ebionite Jewish Christianity which insisted that Jesus was a man anointed Messiah at his baptism.[40] Kayser next describes other elements in the Testaments which confirm its Ebionite Jewish-Christian origin.[41] Among these are the parallel between Moses and Jesus found in T Levi 8 and the Recognitions (Recog. I.41, 57), the Ebionite view that Jesus is the "only born prophet" found in T Benj 9, the priestly view of Jesus throughout the Testaments, and the use of salt (Clementine Homilies XIV.1) in the Eucharist. Against Ritschl, who saw a positive view of Paul in T Benj 11, Kayser argues that these verses are an interpolation.[42] Moreover, the absence of specific reference to cultic law, circumcision, and sabbath means only that the writer assumed them.[43]

Thus, in a very carefully argued article Kayser refuted the position of Ritschl that the Testaments was the product of Gentile Christianity. He did not argue that Gentile-Christian elements were lacking but that they were secondarily added. For the future, however, Kayser's work will be important, not only for its conclusions, but also for its method. While Grabe had argued for interpolations only along the most primitive literary-critical lines, Kayser employed literary criticism with such precision as to deserve the credit for introducing this method to Testaments study.

Regardless of the merit of Kayser's work, however, it was not successful in convincing J. M. Vorstman[44] that the Gentile-Christian materials in the Testaments were interpolations. Vorstman begins his study of the Testaments with a discussion of its original language. The presence of Greek paronomasia and philosophical vocabulary, the fact that $\delta\iota\alpha\theta\acute{\eta}\kappa\eta$ has no Hebrew equivalent, the use of $\beta\epsilon\lambda\acute{\iota}\alpha\rho$ instead of the Hebrew transliteration $\beta\epsilon\lambda\acute{\iota}\alpha\lambda$, the use of such common Greek forms as μελλεῖν and the genitive absolute, and the appearance of the LXX in T Judah 24, all lead Vorstman to the conclusion that the Testaments was written originally in Greek.[45]

Then, second, concerning its date of writing, Vorstman argues that the terminus post quem is the fall of the Temple and the rise, at the same time, of the Gentile majority within the Church. The terminus ad quem is 135 C.E., because the priestly concern of the Testaments would make no sense after that date. Vorstman prefers a date nearer 70 than 135 C.E., however, since the fall is important within the Testaments and only Paul's first letter (1 Thes 2:16/T Levi 6:11) is used by it.[46]

Third, about the purpose behind the Testaments, Vorstman says that this document was written to convert the Jews to Christianity by appealing to their own Fathers, Abraham's children.[47]

Vorstman's major concern in the first part of his study is nonetheless the authorship of the Testaments. Kayser had argued that the author was a Jewish Christian because he betrayed no elements of Pauline Christianity. Kayser had admitted, however, that T Benj 11 praised Paul, although he insisted that these verses were an interpolation. But now Vorstman defends the basic integrity of just these verses and concludes that they are proof of the Pauline-Christian authorship of the Testaments.[48] He next indicates that various other Pauline themes (the new priest, universalism, the Messiah's law) are present in the document,[49] while certain characteristic Jewish-Christian motifs (chiliasm, asceticism) are absent.[50] On the basis of this evidence, then, Vorstman affirms Ritschl's theory that the Testaments is Gentile-Christian in origin.[51]

The second part of Vorstman's work is a discussion of the Testaments in terms of its value in the history of apocalyptic, dogmatics, and moral doctrine. Of particular interest here is Vorstman's contention (against Kayser) that the patripassionistic christological elements in the Testaments are not only integral to the document but also form a far larger body of material than that referring to Jesus' humanity.[52]

Although Vorstman had presented a concerted defense of Ritschl's position, Ritschl himself in the same year reversed his previous opinion and accepted the view of Kayser that the Testaments was a product of Jewish Christianity![53] Against Kayser, however, Ritschl argues that the Testaments was not the work of an Ebionite Jewish Christian, i.e., with nationalistic, anti-universal, ascetic, legalistic tendencies, and low christology, but of a more orthodox Nazarene Jewish Christian open to the Gentiles and with a positive view of Paul. Hence, according to Ritschl the T Benj 11 passage is not necessarily an interpolation.

What made Ritschl change his mind? The Testaments has a strong concern for the conversion of the Jews.[54] This must have disappeared very early from the Gentile-Christian Church and maintained itself only among Jewish Christians.[55]

But agreement on the Jewish-Christian authorship of the Testaments was by no means universal. A. Hilgenfeld[56] closed out the decade of the 1850s with an article rejecting the new position of Ritschl. Referring again to T Benj 11, Hilgenfeld argues that this was written by a Gentile Christian.[57] Moreover, he argues that the Gentile Christians had long been concerned with the conversion of Israel.[58] And beyond this, he asserts that a Jewish Christian could not have written the anti-Jewish polemic which permeates the Testaments.[59] The extensive Jewish materials in the document show that it was written by a Jew who had become a Pauline Christian.[60] This helps to explain the few cases of a "low" christology found in the Testaments.[61]

Thus we see that the decade of the 1850s was very active in its discussion of the authorship of the Testaments. All of the scholars involved were agreed that it was a Christian writing, ca. 70-135 C.E. But among them there was no consensus concerning the Christian author. Was he a Pauline, Gentile Christian? Was he a Jewish Christian, Ebionite, or Nazarene? Even if Ritschl had changed his mind, Vorstman and Hilgenfeld nonetheless remained convinced that the writer was a Pauline Christian. And even if Kayser had shown specific grounds for his supposed interpolations, he was not followed by any other scholar of the period. Hilgenfeld was able to recognize patripassionistic and Ebionite christological elements in the Testaments without seeing any major difficulty in these. Thus, the decade closed with the major problem of origins unresolved, although a consensus had developed in terms of language (Greek), date (70-135 C.E.), and purpose (the conversion of the Jews).

The 1850s set the terms of discussion for the next two and a half decades. Although no subsequent decade of the nineteenth century produced as much study as the 1850s, the following years saw significant research on the Testaments as well as the creation of a scholarly consensus concerning its origin.

Discussion of the Testaments began slowly in the 1860s,[62] but in 1866 J. Langen[63] did take up the topic. Against Grabe's contention that this was originally a Jewish document written in Hebrew, Langen affirms that the Christian materials within it are contextually necessary,[64] and that the arguments of Nitzsch and Vorstman prove Greek to be its original language.[65] Against Nitzsch, however, he argues that the Testaments was not written in Alexandria but in Palestine, since the fall of the Temple, so important to the Testaments, was a particularly Palestinian concern. Nor is the Greek language of the Testaments a problem to this theory, because Greek was used by the Jews in Palestine.[66]

Concerning the date of writing, Langen is in general agreement with previous scholars, but suggests that the terminus ad quem is provided by the lack of reference to the troubles of Palestine under Hadrian. The Testaments was written, therefore, between 70 and ca. 110 C.E.[67]

Finally, Langen takes up the main issue of the 1850s, saying that he can find none of the many interpolations discovered by Kayser. He does agree with Ritschl, however, that the writer of the Testaments was a Jewish Christian open to Paulinism.[68] Nonetheless, the significance of Langen's analysis is not the support he gave to Ritschl's position, but the attempt, unique with the exception of Nitzsch, to find where the Testaments was written.[69]

The major discussion of the Testaments in the 1860s did not appear until the last year of that decade. If the works of Grabe, Corrodi, Nitzsch, Kayser, and Ritschl are landmarks in the history of Testaments research, even more so is that of R. Sinker.[70] The object of his study was the presentation of a complete introduction and text, based upon the two Greek MSS known to him at that time.

Sinker begins by offering a study "On the Parties of the Early Church," especially the Nazarene Jewish Christians.[71] In discussing the authorship of the Testaments, he comes to the same conclusion as Ritschl that the Testaments is the product of Nazarene Jewish Christianity.[7] It is Jewish-Christian because it emphasizes Levi, maintains the Law and Jewish morality in general, is Jewish in its theme, i. e., the Patriarchs, and has elements of Jewish-Christian christology. And the Testaments is Nazarene rather than Ebionite because it is universal in outlook.

Sinker is in general agreement with scholars before him in dating the Testaments after 70 C.E. and before 135, although his reasons for so doing are somewhat different. His terminus ad quem is based on the priestly elements in the Testaments which would not be present after 135 C.E. His terminus post quem is based upon three elements within the Testaments, i.e., an apparently Gentile majority in the Church, an incarnational theology, and familiarity with a nearly complete New Testament canon.[73]

Finally, a significant part of this study is Sinker's discussion "On the Christology of the Testaments." Here he refutes the position of Kayser that the christology of the Testaments reveals the interpolative nature of the document as a whole. Thus, according to Sinker,

> much there is which seems contradictory, and hence the theory of interpolation has constantly been called in, but it seems fair to ask whether some of the cases, at any rate, may not be referred to the reason above stated, that the author is not writing a theological code, but a religious essay in popular form.[74]

He then examines the two different sets of passages which stress Jesus' human and divine nature. His conclusion: within the former there is a recognition of the latter.[75] And concerning the relationship between God and the Son in the Testaments, he reaches the following result:

> It is thus readily seen of how fluctuating a nature was the Nazarene theology on this point, and this may account for what otherwise would be a puzzling phenomenon in the Testaments, the concurrent identification of Christ with God and His distinction from Him.[76]

After a brief discussion of the person of Christ and ethics in the Testaments, Sinker offers his concluding description of its origin. He sees a

Nazarene Jewish Christian, in the period after Titus but before Bar-Cochba, writing from Pella as a part of a "gentle, recluse body, displaying many of the features that shed so great a charm over the Judaism of the day."[77] It is this description which is the great merit of Sinker's work. Sinker had not discovered exceptional evidence for the resolution of introductory problems, but he had listened for the voice of a particular people in a particular time. He heard it and so allowed the Testaments in all of its humanness to speak again from Pella and the Christians there.

A. Geiger also wrote about the Testaments in 1869.[78] According to him it is an uninterpolated Jewish-Christian work differing only from a purely Jewish writing in its designation of Jesus as the Messiah.[79] In determining the type of Jewish Christian who wrote the Testaments, Geiger distinguishes the Pharisaic from the Sadducean Jewish Christians. The former stressed the Law and the resurrection of Jesus; the latter, as in the Epistle to the Hebrews, Jesus' priesthood. Geiger sees in the Testaments a clear witness to this latter Sadducean group.[80]

A final point of interest in Geiger's study is the evidence which he finds in T Judah 26 for the dating of the Testaments.[81] In that chapter Judah asks not to be buried in costly garments. According to Geiger this request must reflect the ruling of Gamaliel I shortly before the fall of the Temple that such garments not be used for burial. Therefore, T Judah 26 indicates that the Testaments was written soon after the ruling was made. Moreover, because after the fall of the Temple there was no need for the request since all were buried poor, the Testaments must have been written before 70 C.E. Thus, Geiger establishes a new terminus post quem and ad quem; he dates the Testaments in the years just before the destruction of the Temple.

Although the decade of the 1860s had not resolved the question of the origin of the Testaments, it is clear that the consensus now favored a Jewish-Christian milieu. In the next thirteen years from 1870 to 1883 this consensus is further confirmed.

In 1870 F. Nitzsch[82] wrote very briefly on the Testaments in agreement with Ritschl that its writer was a non-Ebionite, pro-Pauline Jewish Christian. He is a Jewish Christian because only this group wished to convert Israel; he is not an Ebionite because he speaks well of Paul and avoids the ceremonial Law for the Gentiles. The use of Revelation, James, and Hebrews indicates a terminus post quem of 100 C.E. The openness between Jew and Christian and the pre-Hadrian remnant of the Jewish nation establish a terminus ad quem between 110 and 135 C.E.

However, in an 1871 review of Sinker's book, A. Hilgenfeld[83] repeated his 1858 arguments against the Jewish-Christian authorship of the Testaments. Granted that it has a Jewish audience, the purpose of the document is not to convert but to dispute and do battle with this audience. Specifically, the Testaments fights the Jews of Jamnia (T Naph 6); and the patripassionism of the work could not be the product of any form of Jewish Christianity.

Unlike the 1850s, however, there was now no other support forthcoming for Hilgenfeld's position.[84] In 1874[85] E. Reuss agreed with Ewald (see note 69) that the writer was a man of levitical spirit; but against Ewald he argued that, since T Benj 11 is unique in the Testaments in its pro-Paulinism, the Testaments must be a Jewish-Christian work with these verses interpolated. In 1880 B. B. Warfield[86] described Testaments as a Nazarene Jewish-Christian document written at Pella before 117 c. e. Again, shortly thereafter, A. Dillmann[87] published a review of research, concluding that the Testaments was the work of a pro-Pauline Jewish Christian; and so similarly, B. Pick.[88]

The years from 1870 to 1883 contributed little to original research on the Testaments. Nonetheless, while they did not offer new evidence concerning the question of origins, they did reflect the development of a consensus out of the debates of the 1850s and 1860s. This consensus was nearly fixed in the 1870s, and in the early 1880s Warfield, Dillmann, and Pick affirmed it with their agreement that the Testaments was a Jewish-Christian document, not Ebionite but open to the Gentile Church.

Thus, by the 1880s scholars had developed their thesis of Nazarene-Christian origins to its logical conclusion. Corrodi and Nitzsch showed that the Testaments was a Christian document, Kayser that it was Jewish-Christian, and Ritschl and Sinker that it was Nazarene Jewish-Christian. Having reached this consensus, where was scholarship now to go? Certainly its likely direction was in using the Testaments as a rare and valuable primary source for uncovering the mysteries of early Jewish Christianity. Such did not happen, however. The Testaments was never allowed to speak from this perspective, for with the publication in 1884 of Friedrich Schnapp's literary-critical study of the Testaments, the developing consensus of the past two hundred years was suddenly reversed. Grabe had been right all along.

In our next chapter, therefore, we deal with the rapid rise of a new consensus.

FOOTNOTES

[1]Jürgen Becker, *Untersuchungen zur Entstehungsgeschichte der Testamente der zwölf Patriarchen* (Leiden: E. J. Brill, 1970) 129.

[2]Johannes Ernestus Grabius (ed.), *Spicilegium SS. Patrum ut et Haereticorum, seculi post Christum natum I. II.& III* (Oxford: [n.n.], 1698) 1. 29.

[3]Friedrich Schnapp, *Die Testamente der zwölf Patriarchen untersucht* (Halle: Max Niemeyer, 1884) 7-13.

[4]R. H. Charles (ed.), *The Testaments of the Twelve Patriarchs, Translated from the Editor's Greek Text* (London: Adam and Charles Black, 1908) xxxviii-xli. But notice also in the same author's *The Apocrypha and Pseudepigrapha of the Old Testament* (Oxford: Clarendon, 1913) 2.295, Charles jumped in Section C from Grabe to Schnapp with no mention of the long intervening period from 1698 to 1883.

[5]Matthew Paris, *Chronica Majora* (ed. Henry Richards Luard; London: Longman and Co., 1877) 4.232-33.

[6]*Testamenta duodecim Patriarchu filiorum Jacob e greco in latinu versa; Roberto Linconiensi Episcopo interprete.* This text names no printer nor place and time of writing. According to Robert Sinker, *Testamenta XII Patriarcharum: Appendix* (Cambridge: Deighton, Bell and Co., 1879) 10, this is the *editio princeps* of the Latin Version. The copy I used is that owned by Union Theological Seminary in New York City.

[7]*Testament und Abschrifft der zwölf Patriarchen der Söhnen Jacobs* ([n.p.]: Menradi Molteri und Augustini Lantzkroni, 1544) 2-4.

[8]So Charles (ed.), *The Testaments of the Twelve Patriarchs* xxi, noted a 17th century Greek MS with an introduction stating that John Chrysostom translated the Testaments from Hebrew to Greek. Similarly, Robert Sinker (*The Testaments of the XII Patriarchs* [Cambridge: Deighton, Bell and Co., 1869] xii and xiv) mentioned two Latin MSS of the 15th century with the same statement.

[9]Grabe. *Spicilegium SS. Patrum* 1. 129-44.

[10]Ibid., 133. See T Sim 5:4-6.

[11]Ibid., 135-38.

[12]Ibid., 134.

[13]Ibid., 135, 138. Compare 1 Thes 2:16 with T Levi 6:11.

[14]Ibid., 139-40. The terminus ad quem is (p. 131) Origen's "Homilia xv. in Josuam" where the title of the Testaments is cited. Grabe also mentions Tertullian's "contra Marcionem" as having a possible reference to T Benj 11:1. The former reference has become the standard evidence for the terminus ad quem. The latter (Adv. Marc. V.1), if correct (and if referring to St. Paul as Grabe and most subsequent scholars have thought), would indicate that at least a part of the Christian elements in the Testaments was present prior to Tertullian.

[15]Grabe, *Spicilegium SS. Patrum* 1. 143.

[16]The pre-Grabe period was not totally unanimous, for Grabe himself mentions two scholars, Dodwell and Cave, who had considered the Testaments a Greek-language Christian writing. I have been unable to trace Grabe's citations.

[17]J.-P. Migne (ed.), *Patrologiae cursus completus. Series graeca* (Paris: Paul Dupont, 1886) 2. 1024-1030.

[18]Johan. Albertus Fabricius (ed.), *Codex pseudepigraphus Veteris Testamenti* (2nd ed.; Hamburg: Theodori Christoph. Felginer, 1722) 1. 759. The first edition appeared in 1713.

[19]This is with the exception of Nathaniel Lardner, *The Credibility of the Gospel History* (London: [n.n.], 1735) 741-81. Lardner offered excerpts of the Testaments combined with sermonic comments. Of value is his assertion (pp. 745-46) that this document speaks positively of the Gentiles.

[20]Andrea Gallandi (ed.), *Bibliotheca veterum patrum* (Venice: Joannio Baptistae Albrittii Hieron., 1765) 1. li-liv.

[21][Heinrich Corrodi], *Kritische Geschichte des Chiliasmus* (Leipzig: [n.n.], 1781) 2. 101-103.

[22]Carolus Immanuel Nitzsch, *De Testamentis duodecim Patriarchorum libro V.T. Pseudepigrapho* (Wittenberg: ex officina typographica Friderici Immanuelis Siebt., 1810) 1-13. Union Theological Seminary (N.Y.) now possesses a microfilm of this work.

[23]Ibid., 13.

[24]Ibid., 16.

[25]Ibid.

[26]Ibid., 17.

[27]Ibid., 17-27.

[28]I. A. Dorner, *History of the Development of the Doctrine of the Person of Christ* (Edinburgh: T. and T. Clark, 1861) 1. 155.

[29]Ibid., 1. 160.

[30]Ibid., 1. 156.

[31]Albrecht Ritschl, *Die Entstehung der altkatholischen Kirche* (Bonn: Adolph Marcus, 1850) 324-25.

[32]A. Kayser, "Die Testamente der XII Patriarchen," *Beiträge zu den theologischen Wissenschaften in Verbindung mit der theologischen Gesellschaft zu Strassburg* (1851) 3. 107-140.

[33]Ibid., 107-09.

[34]Ibid., 110.

[35]Ibid., 112.

[36]Ibid.

[37]Ibid., 113.

[38]Ibid., 113-14.

[39]Ibid., 114.

[40]Ibid., 115-18.

[41]Ibid., 119-20, 128.

[42]Ibid., 139-40.

[43]Ibid., 124.

[44]Johannes Marinus Vorstman, *Disquisitio de Testamentorum XII Patriarcharum* (Rotterdam: P. C. Hoog, 1857).

[45]Ibid., 7-12.

[46]Ibid., 13-26.

[47]Ibid., 26-29.

[48]Ibid., 35-36.

[49]Ibid., 43.

[50]Ibid., 44-48.

[51]Ibid., 51.

[52]Ibid., 68-75.

[53]Albrecht Ritschl, *Die Entstehung der altkatholischen Kirche* (2nd ed.; Bonn: Adolph Marcus, 1857) 171-77.

[54]Ibid., 172.

[55]Ibid.

[56]A. Hilgenfeld, "Das Urchristentum und seine neuesten Bearbeitungen von Lechler und Ritschl," *Zeitschrift für wissenschaftliche Theologie* 1 (1858) 377-440.

[57]Ibid., 395.

[58]Ibid., 396.

[59]Ibid., 397.

[60]Ibid., 396.

[61]Ibid., 398.

[62]In 1860 W. A. van Hengel (*De Testamenten der twaalf Patriarchen* [Amsterdam: Ten Brink & de Vries]) published a history of research dealing thoroughly with Vorstman's work.

[63]Joseph Langen, *Das Judenthum in Palästina zur Zeit Christi* (Freiburg: Herder'sche Verlagshandlung, 1866) 140-57.

[64]Ibid., 144.

[65]Ibid., 143.

[66]Ibid. Moreover, the stress of the Testaments on history rather than allegory indicates its Palestinian rather than Alexandrian place of origin.

[67]Ibid., 146-47.

[68]Ibid., 149-54.

[69]Two years later, Heinrich Ewald (*Geschichte des Volkes Israel* [3rd ed.; Göttingen: Dieterichsche Buchhandlung. 1868] 7. 361-66) repeated the position of Vorstman and Hilgenfeld that T Benj 11 proved the Gentile-Christian authorship of the Testaments.

[70]Robert Sinker, *The Testaments of the XII Patriarchs* (Cambridge: Deighton, Bell and Co., 1869). Ten years later Sinker published his *Testamenta XII Patriarcharum: Appendix* (Cambridge: Deighton, Bell and Co., 1879). The former contains (pp. 129-201) the Greek text according to Cambridge University Library MS Ff I.24 with variant readings provided by the Oxford (Bodleian) Library MS Barocci 133. The latter gives a collation of two further MSS (Vatican Library Cod. Graec. 731 and Library of the Monastery of St. John the Evangelist [Patmos] Cod. 411) with MS Ff I.24.

[71]Sinker, *Testaments* (1869) 8-16.

[72]Ibid., 16-28.

[73]Ibid., 28-29.

[74]Ibid., 89.

[75]Ibid., 93.

[76]Ibid., 103.

[77]Ibid., 123.

[78]Abraham Geiger, "Apokryphen zweiter Ordnung," *Jüdische Zeitschrift für Wissenschaft und Leben* 7 (1869) 116-35.

[79]Ibid., 116.

[80]Ibid., 119-31.

[81]Ibid., 133.

[82]Friedrich Nitzsch, *Grundriss der christlichen Dogmengeschichte* (Berlin: Mittler und Sohn, 1870) 109-11.

[83]A. Hilgenfeld, rev. of Robert Sinker, *Testaments*, in *Zeitschrift für wissenschaftliche Theologie* 14 (1871) 302-05.

[84]This is with the exception of Ernest Renan (*Histoire des origines du christianisme: L'église chrétienne* [Paris: Michel Lévy Fréres, 1879] 268-70), who said the Testaments was the work of a Jew who had become a Pauline Christian. It was written in Judea, in a semitic Greek, against the Jews.

[85]E. Reuss, *Die Geschichte der heiligen Schriften Neuen Testaments* (5th ed.; Braunschweig: C. A. Schwetschke und Sohn, 1874) 257, 266.

[86]B. B. Warfield, "The Apologetical Value of the Testaments of the Twelve Patriarchs," *Presbyterian Review* 1 (1880) 58-84.

[87]A. Dillmann, "Pseudepigraphen des Alten Testaments," *Real-Encyclopädie für protestantische Theologie und Kirche* 12 (1883) 361-62.

[88]B. Pick, "The Testaments of the Twelve Patriarchs," *Lutheran Church Review* 4 (1885) 161-86.

CHAPTER III

The Testaments of the Twelve Patriarchs and the Period from 1884 to 1908: A New Consensus Is Reached

Jürgen Becker's history of research on the Testaments really starts with the period begun by F. Schnapp. Becker justifies this by the statement that the earlier period "bringt keine literarkritisch verwendbaren Gesichtspunkte, ist jedoch typisch für ein bis heute zu beobachtendes Gesetz: Wer die christliche Verfasserschaft vertritt, muss mit literarischer Einheitlichkeit rechnen."[1] Of course, this statement is not accurate because we have already shown in the discussion of the 1850s that the work of Kayser was primarily literary-critical; and it argued against the unity of the Testaments. Again, the whole question of the Paulinism of the Testaments, especially as it related to T Benj 11, dealt with the possibility of disunity on literary-critical grounds. It is accurate to say, however, that Becker's history concerns itself primarily with literary-critical endeavors, and particularly with those which seek to show that the Christian materials in the Testaments are interpolations in the Jewish original. Such a tendency appears also in Becker's jump from Grabe's interpolation theory to that of Schnapp two centuries later without any consideration of the intervening period. It is important to mention this now because otherwise the shadow of uniformity is spread over the period 1698 to 1908 in which, as we have shown in the first chapter, such a uniformity did not exist.

But if there was no uniformity over the period from 1698 to 1908, there was a consensus concerning Christian authorship of the Testaments between 1700 and 1884; and there was from the 1850s until 1884 a growing consensus of Nazarene or orthodox Jewish-Christian authorship. However, such a radical change took place in 1884 with the publication of Friedrich Schnapp's monograph[2] that a completely new consensus was created between 1884 and the publication of R. H. Charles' editions of the Testaments in 1908. This consensus has dominated Testaments study to the present day. Starting with Schnapp we shall now describe the rise of this new consensus between 1884 and 1908.

Schnapp and Literary Criticism

The key to Schnapp's method is described in his introduction.[3] After discussing the previous history of research and the arguments of those who supported the Pauline- and Jewish-Christian authorship of the Testaments,[4] Schnapp argues, in agreement with Kayser, that the divergent opinions about the authorship of the document rest upon the presence of contradictory materials within it. Many who had seen a Jewish-Christian author omitted reference to T Benj 11. Similarly, Kayser had omitted all patripassionistic elements as later interpolations. From this need of scholars to omit various parts of the Testaments in order to avoid contradictions within its text, Schnapp concludes that it is not a unity but a work interpolated by secondary hands.[5]

How are we to discover what materials are interpolated? Langen had argued that internal evidence alone was too subjective. According to Schnapp this is not so. Rather, a purely literary-critical method based upon the discovery of inner contradictions is the necessary tool for the recovery of the original text and the discovery of the layer(s) of interpolation.[6]

In order to establish guidelines for the discovery of these interpolations Schnapp works very closely with T Levi,[7] applying his conclusions from that section of the Testaments to all of the others. His first observation is that T Levi's introduction is atypical of the introductions to the other testaments because it concerns itself with the future whereas the others deal only with ethical exhortation. Therefore, Schnapp concludes that the future-oriented introduction to T Levi must be an interpolation.[8]

Next, Schnapp observes that T Levi 2-5 has this same future orientation in strong contrast to T Levi 6. This leads him to conclude that T Levi 2-5 is also interpolated.[9] But beyond this, T Levi 2-5 contains material of a clearly Christian nature.[10] Schnapp then works through the rest of T Levi in a similar manner finding that the original testament ended after T Levi 13. T Levi 8, 10, 14-19 all display a strong future orientation and contain Christian materials.[11]

From this analysis he comes to the following conclusions: first, the original Testaments focused upon moral exhortation derived from the lives of the Patriarchs.[12] Second, to this original document Jewish apocalyptic materials had been added.[13] Third, into these Jewish apocalyptic additions Christian materials have been interpolated.[14] Schnapp then applies these results to the rest of the Testaments, finding that only in T Gad is the original document preserved.[15]

The work of Schnapp must not be underestimated. He had established along literary-critical lines the theory first proposed by Grabe in 1698. Later scholars do not all agree with his specific results but very few disagree with his basic conclusion that the Testaments is a Jewish writing with various interpolations; his literary-critical method appears again and again.

B. Pick,[16] who wrote after the publication of Schnapp's study, was evidently not aware of it and we have mentioned him therefore under the previous period. But the next discussion of the Testaments, that of J. M. S. Baljon,[17] was very much aware of Schnapp and set the tone for the acceptance of his views. Baljon credits Grabe and Kayser with establishing an interest in interpolation theories.[18] In his affirmation of the views of Schnapp,[19] he presents what he considers to be the Jewish and Christian interpolations.[20] Just as with Schnapp, the latter consistently come within the former.

Baljon was first in acknowledging Schnapp's basic theory. Not until between 1886 and 1891, however, did this theory receive the wide hearing it deserved. This happened when it was publicized in E. Schürer's extensive Jewish history.[21] In his discussion of Palestinian Jewish literature Schürer accepts Schnapp's position. He affirms the three levels of material without additional evidence,[22] and rejects the possibility of a Christian origin for the Testaments with the argument that no Christian could affirm Levi-Judah as rulers since it was they who had persecuted Jesus.[23] Moving beyond Schnapp, Schürer deals once more with the question of the type of Christians who had interpolated the Jewish document, arguing from the elements of universalism and patripassionism that they were Gentiles.[24] He also suggests that the Christian interpolations are more extensive than had been indicated by Schnapp.[25]

Schürer's discussion of the Testaments was not intended as a thorough analysis. But in the popularization and acceptance which it gave to Schnapp, it appears to have been a major factor in subsequent research. After its publication only very lonely voices were raised in favor of the consensus reached prior to 1884.

The first of these lonely voices appeared in W. J. Deane's *Pseudepigrapha*.[26] He argues against Schnapp on the grounds of both method and content. Concerning method, Deane says that Schnapp started with a preconceived notion about the nature of the Testaments and then marked as interpolation everything which did not conform to his notion. Specifically, Deane argues that a text cannot be called interpolated unless first, there are clear sutures; second, the style and language in the supposed interpolation differ from the rest of the document; and third, the MSS are at wide variance from each other. He then concludes that since none of these conditions applies to the Testaments, the interpolation theory is doubtful.[27]

Concerning content, Deane argues that the Testaments is replete with references to the New Testament.[28] As a literary unity, therefore, it is a Nazarene Jewish-Christian document.[29] Apparent disagreements in christology reflect the early date of Testaments compilation.[30]

But Deane's was an unheard voice. In 1892 E. de Faye[31] summarized and accepted the views presented by Schnapp and affirmed by Schürer, as did K. Kohler.[32] Beyond this, however, Kohler uses T Levi as evidence that the Testaments was written during the period of John Hyrcanus.[33] Moreover, he argues that it is a Pharisaic document (against Geiger) because of its rich use of angels.[34] Already in 1893, therefore, Kohler presented in a nutshell what was soon to become under R. H. Charles the standard view of the *Sitz im Leben* of the Testaments within the new consensus. Nor is there any doubt that by 1893 such a consensus was already in existence; and it depended upon the literary criticism of F. Schnapp.

Conybeare and Text Criticism

Modern research, however, with its view of an original Jewish Testaments behind the present document, is dependent not only upon the literary-critical method but also, and equally, upon text criticism. In 1893 this method made its appearance in a very important article by F. C. Conybeare.[35] The topic of his article is the discovery in 1891 of the Edschmiadzin MS of the Bible containing the Armenian Version of the Testaments.

According to Conybeare this MS offers a text of the Testaments free of much of the Christian material found in the Sinker Greek edition of 1869; it thus supports the theory of Grabe worked out on literary-critical grounds by Schnapp.[36] But Conybeare does make three qualifications in the correspondence found between the literary-critically established Jewish Testaments and the Edschmiadzin MS. First, the Edschmiadzin MS has various corruptions.[37] Second, some apparently Christian material is found in the MS.[38] Third, the Armenian MSS of the Mechitarist Congregation in Venice are more strongly "Christianized" than is the Edschmiadzin MS.[39] However, while Conybeare was careful to make the above qualifications, it was still the central thrust of his keynote article that the discovery of this Armenian MS provided the necessary external evidence in confirmation of Schnapp's literary-critical theory.[40]

Gaster and the Beginnings of Source Criticism

If between them Schnapp and Conybeare had established what appeared to be an impenetrable wall against the theory of Christian origins, an article in 1894 by M. Gaster was so much more cement for the wall.[41] In a thirteenth century MS of the Chronicle of Jerahmeel,[42] Gaster believed that he had found the Hebrew original of T Naphtali. Before discussing his find, however, Gaster makes two general observations about the Testaments. First, because it contains so much Jewish tradition it must be of Jewish origin.[43] Second, it was written originally in Hebrew. Not only is this the language of the Patriarchs, but also the Greek Testaments shows clear signs of Hebrew mistranslation.[44] Thus, Gaster here asserts what Grabe had claimed long ago, and at the same time points the way to the development of specific evidence, as in R. H. Charles later, of the original language of the Testaments.

Nonetheless, these observations are only preliminary. Gaster's primary concern is the comparison of the Greek T Naphtali with the Hebrew Chronicle of Jerahmeel. The Greek text is not only difficult to understand when compared to the Hebrew, but appears also to be enlarged with Christian materials.[45] It is, therefore, secondary to and dependent upon the original Hebrew T Naphtali of the Chronicle.[46]

Harnack and the Gathering of Literary-, Text-, and Source-Critical Forces

In 1897 the first volume appeared of the second part of A. Harnack's *Geschichte der altchristlichen Literatur bis Eusebius*. Here Harnack described the state of Testaments research at the end of the nineteenth century and also brought together the various forces mustered over the previous few years for the defense of the Jewish origin of the Testaments.[47]

According to Harnack the thesis of the Jewish origin of the Testaments is correct on literary-critical grounds for two reasons. First, most of the material in the Testaments is Jewish;[48] second, the Christian material appears in the Jewish interpolations as described by Schnapp.[49] Again, the thesis is correct on text-critical grounds because the Armenian Version does show a less Christianized Testaments.[50] Finally, it is correct on source-critical grounds because Gaster's discovery shows that there does exist a Jewish work behind the present Testaments in which, just as Schnapp had said, the eschatological materials are absent.[51] Harnack then discusses the Christian materials in the Testaments, noting that the modalistic and Ebionite christological elements prove two stages of Christian interpolation but make a definite dating of these stages impossible.[52] Concerning the Jewish original, Harnack says only that it must have been written at about the same time as Jubilees, perhaps at the beginning of the Christian era.[53]

Two years later R. H. Charles, a man whose work is to have lasting significance, wrote his first article on the Testaments. In 1899 Charles[54] affirms the work done by Schnapp with its conclusions about Jewish and Christian interpolation. At the same time, he argues for different stages of Christian interpolation, using Conybeare's Armenian MS as a witness to an early stage.[55] Charles is also concerned with the question of the original language of the document.[56] At this point he brings Gaster's Hebrew T Naphtali into the discussion. This document is not the source of T Naphtali in the Testaments. It is not only very late and "probably composed long after the Christian era," but also differs greatly from the Greek T Naphtali.[57] Nonetheless, both the Greek and the Hebrew texts appear to go back to common Hebrew traditions; to this extent Gaster's text is evidence that the Testaments was written originally in Hebrew. And there is even more conclusive evidence of this, based upon the Greek text itself. First, the Greek often uses Hebrew constructions; second, upon retranslation it shows signs of Hebrew paronomasia; and third, the same retranslation clarifies various obscure passages in the Greek.

Thus in 1899 R. H. Charles had begun to bring together his evidence in defense of the Jewish origin of the Testaments. Although he rejected Gaster's claim that the Hebrew T Naphtali was the Jewish original of the interpolated Greek T Naphtali, he did use Gaster's find as a clue to the language of the Testaments and as a witness to earlier sources which went into the writing of the original.

In the same year, another discussion of the Gaster T Naphtali appeared. In a careful comparison of the Hebrew and Greek T Naphtali, G. Resch sought to show that Gaster had been correct in his assertions.[58] According to Resch the Greek T Naphtali has various readings which can be made sense of only when retranslated into Hebrew.[59] Moreover, the entire Greek T Naphtali appears disorganized when compared to the Hebrew; in fact, the Greek text has been interpolated drastically by Christian hands.[60] On the basis of these observations, Resch comes to two main conclusions. First, the Testaments was written originally in Hebrew; second, each testament (like T Naphtali) has been redacted thoroughly by a Christian.[61]

Resch was thus quite sure that Gaster's text had proven the literary-critical theories of Schnapp. But in 1900 Schnapp himself denied the worth of the Hebrew T Naphtali for source criticism of the Testaments![62] Like Charles, Schnapp argues that the two T Naphtalis are so different that the Greek could not be derived from the Hebrew text. Unlike Charles, Schnapp suggests that the Hebrew text is a later reworking of the Greek T Naphtali of the Testaments.[63]

Then in the same year another source appeared which had a direct bearing on Testaments research. This time it was an Aramaic text paralleling Greek T Levi 9-13, found by Schechter in the Cairo Genizah and now partially published by H. L. Pass and J. Arendzen along with the Greek parallels.[64] According to Pass and Arendzen the Greek and Aramaic have a "common origin."[65]

Yet the year 1900 had still not had its last word about the Testaments, because two major articles by W. Bousset and E. Preuschen were yet to appear in the first volume of the *ZNW*.

Preuschen's article[66] is a study of the history of transmission of the Armenian Version of the Testaments, based upon Conybeare's MS[67] and those of the Mechitarists in Venice.[68] According to Preuschen, the Armenian Version came into existence in the fifth or sixth century as a translation from Greek.[69] More important, the witnesses to this version fall into two groups, Group α and Group β, of which the former is the shorter.[70] Preuschen offers a German translation of T Levi from Group β with the Group α omissions indicated in italics.[71] The differences between α and β lead to Preuschen's main question: which text tradition is earlier?

To answer this question he makes the following observations. First, Group α and β are similar in their readings where no omission is involved. Therefore, one must be dependent upon the other.[72] Second, since T Judah in Group α is not shorter than the T Judah of Group β, Group α reveals no tendency toward shortening the text. Therefore, Group β must be a later reworking of Group α.[73] The shorter Armenian Version is therefore the more original. And because Group β is in fact like the Greek Testaments as we know it, Group α is a witness to an earlier text than was previously known. Moreover, Group α does omit some Christian materials recognized as interpolations; it is not entirely free, however, of Christian elements (T Levi 4 and T Dan 5, for example).[74]

Conybeare's important addition to research on the Testaments was his discovery of the significance of the Armenian Version for the origins question. His work suffered, however, from a lack of precision, because it depended originally upon one MS and did not take careful account of the Mechitarist MSS in Venice except to say that they were more Christianized than his own MS.[75] It is necessary therefore to give major credit to Preuschen for the use of the Armenian Version of the Testaments in later scholarship, since he was the first to focus on the question of the relative value of the groups within this version.

In the same volume W. Bousset offered a three-part article on the Testaments, the first of which[76] used Preuschen's conclusions in order to minimize the Christian interpolations in the Testaments more than Schnapp had done in his German translation.[77] In fact, the discussion is in large measure a criticism of Schnapp for using only literary-critical evidence in his quest of the original Jewish document. Bousset corrects this by an examination of the various textual witnesses available in Greek, Armenian, Slavonic, Latin, and Hebrew.[78]

First, he excludes from the discussion the Slavonic and Latin Versions, because the former is based upon an inferior Greek textual tradition and the latter simply recapitulates the known Greek tradition.[79] Similarly, he omits Gaster's Hebrew T Naphtali because it is not the source of the Greek.[80]

Second, using the remaining witnesses, Bousset reduces Schnapp's Christian interpolations.[81] Among the four Greek MSS he prefers the shorter texts, the Vatican (R) and the Oxford (O), rarely accepting a reading from the Cambridge MS (C) used by Grabe and Sinker.[82] Among the Armenian MSS he prefers the Group α established by Preuschen.[83] On the basis of these MSS Bousset concludes that the Christian interpolations in the Testaments are much fewer and briefer than Schnapp had indicated. According to Bousset the original Jewish document was not much different from the present text,[84] i.e., that constituted by the use of the shortest witnesses, the Greek R and the Armenian Group α.

Now, given the original Jewish text or one near to it, in the second part of his article, Bousset deals with the "Composition and Time of Writing of the Jewish Original."[85] First, he argues that there are no grounds to conclude with Schnapp that the apocalyptic sections of the Testaments are interpolated.[86] But, second, contradictions within the text do reveal the presence of interpolations in the Jewish document. These interpolations concern the figure of Levi. Throughout the Testaments he is described in a positive way. However, examination of T Levi 10, 14-16, T Dan 5, and elsewhere, shows a negative evaluation of the Levi figure. Therefore, Bousset concludes that these latter texts must be interpolated.[87] When were they interpolated? This probably happened in the period of Aristobulus II and Hyrcanus II, during the decline of the Maccabean (Levi) line. The original Testaments was written, therefore, during the earlier, nobler days of the Maccabeans.[88]

Finally, in the third part of his article,[89] Bousset discusses the Aramaic T Levi fragment found by Schechter and made known by Pass and Arendzen. As noted above, Bousset had seen little value in the Gaster Hebrew T Naphtali; this is not true, however, of the Aramaic fragment. According to Bousset, it offers the original text of the Greek T Levi 10.

The work of Preuschen and Bousset will be important for future scholarship. Preuschen preferred the shorter Armenian Version with its limited Christian content, and Bousset affirmed the shortest Greek MSS. Moreover, Bousset sought to discover the earliest form of the Testaments attainable through text criticism and then applied to this text the literary-critical method. In so doing he found no grounds for Schnapp's omission of apocalyptic elements, but did justify omission of part of the Levi materials. In this second matter and in the use he made of it for dating the Jewish Testaments, Bousset has been followed often by subsequent scholarship.

R. H. Charles and the Culmination of the Period 1884-1908

In the years from 1901 to 1907 R. H. Charles wrote three articles on the Testaments. While his 1901[90] contribution offered little beyond what he had already said in 1899, his article of 1904 did move beyond the earlier writing, particularly concerning his theory about the date of the Testaments.[91]

After affirming the value of the Armenian Version as evidence in support of Schnapp's position,[92] Charles once again demonstrates that Hebrew was the original language of the Testaments.[93] The distinctive element in his 1904 article, however, is the establishment of the original date of the Testaments. Specifically, because T Reuben 6:10-11 describes the priest-king figure of the Maccabean period, it must have been composed in that period. Moreover, this figure is highly esteemed in the Testaments. Therefore, because Josephus spoke similarly of John Hyrcanus, our document was written between 135 and 105 B.C.E., during the reign of Hyrcanus. The author was a Pharisee.[94]

Nor were the years 1906-1907 without a contribution from R. H. Charles, this time in company with A. Cowley.[95] H. L. Pass, as already noted, had published an Aramaic fragment of a T Levi.[96] Later, Cowley found another fragment from the same Cairo Genizah deposit which matched in handwriting that published by Pass; and Charles himself had found a Greek addition to T Levi 18:2 in a Mt. Athos MS corresponding in content to the Pass and Cowley Aramaic fragments.[97]

Given this relationship between the Greek interpolation of the Mt. Athos MS and the two Aramaic fragments, Charles and Cowley first seek to show that the same Hebrew original stands behind both the Greek and the Aramaic texts.[98] Then, noting the many differences between the Greek-Aramaic fragments and the T Levi of the Testaments, they conclude that T Levi is not the source reflected in these fragments. Their source is a text which used T Levi freely or was used freely by T Levi. In the opinion of Charles and Cowley, though it is not clear why, the latter is the more likely possibility.[99]

The years 1906 and 1907 still had other contributions to make to work on the Testaments. Kohler, who had written on the Testaments in 1893, now offered a brief summary of research noting that the literary criticism of Schnapp, the textual criticism of Conybeare and the source criticism of Gaster, Pass, and Cowley/Charles had established the Jewish origin of the Testaments.[100] A. Bertholet offered the suggestion that the exhortation of the Testaments derives from the synagogue homily.[101] And A. Schlatter, another of the unheard voices, saw the Testaments in its present form as a Christian document.[102] Finally, I. Lévi built upon the Charles/Cowley article, arguing that it proved the Jewish origin of the Testaments.[103]

Thus, until 1908 R. H. Charles was one of many scholars who had discussed the Testaments with relative brevity; but in that year came the publication of his full introduction and text of the document. This publication remains a monumental event in the history of Testaments research, not only because it still stands as the accepted foundation for study, but also because it took all of the building blocks fashioned from Schnapp onward and constructed from them the critical whole which always will bear Charles' name. It is he who becomes the spokesman for the modern theory of the Jewish authorship of the Testaments developed between 1884 and 1908; and it is his spirit which continues to provide the impetus for critical studies aimed at the final perfection of the Jewish origin theory.

Charles' introduction appears in three different books, *The Greek Versions of the Testaments of the Twelve Patriarchs*,[104] *The Testaments of the Twelve Patriarchs, Translated from the Editor's Greek Text*,[105] both of which appeared in 1908, and *The Apocrypha and Pseudepigrapha of the Old Testament* (1913),[106] which offered an abridged discussion of introductory questions. Since the material is similar in each book, the following summary is taken from the second volume above.

Charles begins his introduction with a presentation of the MSS used in preparing his text of the Testaments,[107] and then describes the two groups of MSS within the Armenian Version, A^α and A^β, of which A^α appears in non-Biblical MSS and A^β in Biblical.[108] While, according to Charles, A^α tends to abbreviate A^β and so cause differences between the two groups, other important differences arise (T Levi 2:7-10 and 16:1,3-5) because the two Armenian groups reflect differences in the two Greek MSS groups, A and B.[109] In general, the Armenian Version as a whole is similar to the Greek Group B and the Slavonic Version. Its major value is that it omits many interpolations of a Christian nature present in the Greek text even though "however valuable A [the Armenian Version in both groups] is, we must not fail to observe that on almost every page it is guilty of unjustifiable omissions."[110]

Thus, although Charles is quick to point out a major weakness of the Armenian Version, he nonetheless uses it in the way spelled out by Conybeare to show text-critically that much of the Christian material in the Testaments is interpolation. While he disagrees with Preuschen's preference for the shorter Armenian Version (A^{α}), he does accept his classification into two groups and in the section T Levi 3:1-5 prefers A^{α} to A^{β} and the Greek text.

Charles next discusses briefly the Slavonic Version and its two MSS groups, noting that the version is late and in general agreement with Greek Group B against Greek Group A.[111] He then describes these two groups within the Greek MSS showing that Greek A is freer from Christian interpolations than Greek B, although Greek A has various errors of omission in its shorter text.[112] Thus, concerning the Greek MSS, Charles approximates closely to the work of Bousset.

He then deals, as he had done in previous articles, with the question of the language of the Jewish original. After noting with amazement that two such important scholars as Sinker and Dillmann had believed the Testaments was written in Greek, Charles credits Kohler with the suggestion that it is a Hebrew language document and Gaster with offering the first attempted proof of this.[113] While he again rejects Gaster's source evidence, he believes there are valid linguistic arguments for the dependence of the present Greek text on an earlier Hebrew one. These arguments are similar to those already presented by Charles in 1899 in his first work on the Testaments.[114] His final concern is to show, using MS evidence, that the two Greek groups do not go back to one original Greek text but rather to two separate Hebrew recensions.[115]

Charles then turns to the date both of the original Hebrew and of the levels of interpolation. Again he argues that the original document was prepared during the period of John Hyrcanus while the Pharisees (who wrote the Testaments) were still strong supporters of Maccabean rule.[116] However, the Testaments also contains much material written against the Maccabees in a fashion similar to that of the Psalms of Solomon. This material can be detected by its negative view of Levi; it was written, therefore, ca. 70-40 B.C.E. as the Pharisees turned away from the corrupt Maccabees.[117]

Charles next discusses the influence of the Testaments upon Jewish[118] and Christian[119] literature by presenting an extensive list of influences on Christianity, but a comparatively minor list for Judaism. Finally, he discusses some of the more important theological elements in the Testaments. The first of these is the conception of forgiveness,[120] about which he had written an article in 1908.[121] His main point is that the Testaments' conception of neighbor-forgiveness is unique in Jewish literature; its only parallel is to be found in the NT. Charles says that

> we have in our text a passage of truly epoch-making importance. Its importance cannot be grasped until we contrast the teaching of the New Testament with that of the Old on the question of man's forgiveness of his neighbor. In the New Testament from the first page to the last it is either explicitly stated or implicitly understood that a man can only receive the divine forgiveness on the condition that he forgives his neighbor. Indeed, in their essential aspects, these two forgivenesses are seen to be one and the same. But in the Old Testament it is very different. There, indeed, God's forgiveness is granted without

money and without price, to the sinner who truly seeks it. But the penitent in the Old Testament could accept and enjoy the divine pardon, and yet cherish the most bitter feelings towards his own personal enemy.[122]

The second theologically important element in the Testaments is its combined concern for the love of God and the love of neighbor. This too is most easily paralleled in the teachings of Jesus.[123] And again, the universalism of the document is certainly not paralleled in Jubilees, a Jewish document contemporary with the Testaments. It is, however, to be found in the New Testament.[124]

Charles at the Center

Looked at from the perspective of the period which we have just discussed, it would appear more proper to entitle this last section of the present chapter "Charles at the End" because Charles' work in 1908 was, as should be clear, the culmination of the work done between 1884 and 1908 by a rather large number of scholars. Little in Charles' work may be attributed solely to him. His general literary-critical evaluation of the Testaments as a Jewish document interpolated by both Jews and Christians goes back directly to Schnapp and before him to Grabe. His separation of pro- and anti-Levi texts used to discover the Jewish interpolations depends upon Bousset; and so too his method of dating the Testaments based upon these Levi elements. Again, Charles' advocacy of the Armenian Version is derived in its basic lines from the work of Preuschen.

Nonetheless, it is still Charles at the center. It is he who gathers all of these diffuse strands, makes this and that alteration and presents as a whole the body of evidence which supports the Jewish origin of the Testaments. And it is he also who, because of the definitive nature of his introduction, comes to be considered *the* authority on the Testaments. In the next chapter we shall see how pervasive was this authority in the period immediately following 1908.

So, then, Charles is at the center. He takes the past to himself and molds from it a way of looking at the Testaments which even now prevails and which, until about 1950, rarely was questioned.

FOOTNOTES

[1]Jürgen Becker, *Untersuchungen zur Entstehungsgeschichte der Testamente der zwölf Patriarchen* (Leiden: E. J. Brill, 1970) 129.

[2]Friedrich Schnapp, *Die Testamente der zwölf Patriarchen untersucht* (Halle: Max Niemeyer, 1884).

[3]Ibid., 1-14.

[4]Ibid., 1-8.

[5]Ibid., 11.

[6]Ibid., 11-14.

[7]Ibid., 14-43.

[8]Ibid., 15-16.

[9]Ibid., 16-18.

[10]Ibid., 23.

[11]Ibid., 23-29.

[12]Ibid., 15.

[13]Ibid., 15-16,42.

[14]Ibid., 23, 28, 29, 31.

[15]Ibid., 73-74.

[16]B. Pick, "The Testaments of the Twelve Patriarchs," *Lutheran Church Review* 4 (1885) 161-86.

[17]J. M. S. Baljon, "De Testamenten der XII Patriarchen," *Theologische Studiën-Utrecht* 4 (1886) 208-31.

[18]Ibid., 214.

[19]Ibid., 214-29.

[20]Ibid., 230.

[21]Emil Schürer, *Geschichte des jüdischen Volkes im Zeitalter Jesu Christi* (Leipzig: J.C. Hinrichs'sche Buchhandlung, 1886-1890). The English translation is *A History of the Jewish People in the Time of Jesus Christ* (New York: Scribner, 1891).

[22]Schürer, *A History of the Jewish People in the Time of Jesus Christ: Second Division* 3. 118-22.

[23]Ibid., 118.

[24]Ibid.

[25]Ibid., 120.

[26]William J. Deane, *Pseudepigrapha* (Edinburgh: T. and T. Clark, 1891) 162-92.

[27]Ibid., 117.

[28]Ibid., 185-90.

[29]Ibid., 178-79.

[30]Ibid., 192.

[31]Eugène de Faye, *Les apocalypses juives: essai de critique littéraire et théologique* (Paris: Georges Bridel, 1892) 217-20.

[32]K. Kohler, "The Pre-Talmudic Haggada," *JQR* 5 (1893) 401.

[33]Ibid., 402.

[34]Ibid., 403. See p. 14 of this study.

[35]Fred. C. Conybeare, "On the Jewish Authorship of the Testaments of the Twelve Patriarchs," *JQR* 5 (1893) 375-98.

[36]Ibid., 382.

[37]Ibid.

[38]Ibid., 396.

[39]Ibid., 397.

[40]Ibid., 383-95.

[41]M. Gaster, "The Hebrew Text of One of the Testaments of the Twelve Patriarchs," *Society of Biblical Archeology: Proceedings* 16-17 (1894) 33-49.

[42]This text in English translation appears in R. H. Charles (ed.), *The Testaments of the Twelve Patriarchs, Translated from the Editor's Greek Text* (London: Adam and Charles Black, 1908) 221-27.

[43]Gaster, "The Hebrew Text of One of the Testaments," 36.

[44]Ibid., 39-40.

[45]Ibid., 42.

[46]Ibid. J. Marshall ("The Hebrew Text of One of the Testaments of the Twelve Patriarchs," *Society of Biblical Archeology: Proceedings* 16-17 [1894] 83-86) immediately affirmed the work of Gaster with its implications of an original Jewish Testaments.

47Adolf Harnack, *Geschichte der altchristlichen Litteratur bis Eusebius* (Leipzig: J. C. Hinrichs'sche Buchhandlung, 1897) 1. 566-70.

48Ibid., 566.

49Ibid., 567.

50Ibid.

51Ibid., 568.

52Ibid., 570.

53Ibid., 566.

54[R. H. Charles], "The Testaments of the XII. Patriarchs," *Encyclopedia Biblica* 1 (1899) 237-41.

55Ibid., 239.

56Ibid., 239-40.

57Charles notes particularly the opposite evaluations of Joseph given in the two documents, i.e., his praise in the Testaments (and Jubilees) and his condemnation in the Gaster text.

58G. Resch, "Das hebräische Testamentum Naphthali," *Theologische Studien and Kritiken* 72 (1899) 206-36.

59Ibid., 227.

60Ibid., 229-31.

61Ibid., 231-36.

62Friedrich Schnapp, "Die Testamente der 12 Patriarchen, der Söhne Jacobs," *Die Apokryphen und Pseudepigraphen des Alten Testaments* (ed. E. Kautzsch; Tübingen: J. C. B. Mohr, 1900) 2. 458-506.

63Ibid., 458-59.

64H. Leonard Pass and J. Arendzen, "Fragment of an Aramaic Text of the Testament of Levi," *JQR* 12 (1900) 651-61. This is the Cambridge fragment.

65Ibid., 652.

66Erwin Preuschen, "Die armenische Übersetzung der Testamente der zwölf Patriarchen," *ZNW* 1 (1900) 106-40.

67See p. 22 of this study.

68Conybeare offered additional Armenian MSS in his "A Collation of Sinker's Texts of the Testaments of Reuben and Simeon with the Old Armenian Version," *JQR* 8 (1896) 260-68; 471-85.

69Preuschen, "Die armenische Übersetzung," 108. Therefore, it pre-dates the earliest Greek MS (Cambridge University Library MS Ff I.24 of the tenth century) by several centuries.

70Ibid., 108-11. In this study the two Armenian groups are designated Group α and Group β (A^α and A^β), and the two Greek groups are designated Group A and Group B.

71Ibid., 112-26.

72Ibid., 127.

73Ibid., 127-30.

74Ibid., 127-29.

75Conybeare, "On the Jewish Authorship," 397.

76W. Bousset, "Die Testamente der XII Patriarchen: I. Die Ausscheidung der christlichen Interpolationen," *ZNW* 1 (1900) 141-75.

77In Kautzsch, *Die Apokryphen und Pseudepigraphen* 460-506.

78Bousset, "Die Testamente," 142.

79Ibid., 144, 145.

80Ibid., 145.

81Ibid., 145-74.

82Ibid., 143. These four Greek MSS appeared in Sinker's work of 1869 and its appendix (1879). They are 1) Cambridge University Library MS Ff I.24; 2) Oxford (Bodleian)Library MS Barocci 133; 3) Vatican Library Cod. Graec. 731; 4) Library of the Monastery of St. John the Evangelist (Patmos) Cod. 411. Sinker called these respectively C,O,R,P. Charles designated them (and so they remain) respectively b,a,c,g.

[83]Ibid., 160.

[84]Ibid., 175.

[85]W. Bousset, "Die Testamente der XII Patriarchen: II. Composition und Zeit der jüdischen Grundschrift," *ZNW* 1 (1900) 187-209.

[86]Ibid., 187.

[87]Ibid., 187-89.

[88]Ibid., 190-202.

[89]W. Bousset, "Ein aramäisches Fragment des Testamentum Levi," *ZNW* 1 (1900) 344-46.

[90]R. H. Charles, "Testaments of the XII Patriarchs," *A Dictionary of the Bible Dealing with Its Language, Literature and Contents* 4 (1909) 721-25. The actual date of the article (p. 725) is 1901 or before. While offering little new concerning the original Jewish writing, this article does list Christian passages in the Testaments which cannot be removed by MS evidence. On the basis of these passages Charles concluded that there was more than one Christian interpolator.

[91][R. H.] Charles, "The Testaments of the XII Patriarchs," *Hibbert Journal* 3 (1904-1905) 558-73.

[92]Ibid., 559-61.

[93]Ibid., 561-64. See also p. 23 of this study.

[94]Ibid., 564-67.

[95]R. H. Charles and A. Cowley, "An Early Source of the Testaments of the Twelve Patriarchs," *JQR* 19 (1907) 566-83.

[96]See p. 24 of the present study.

[97]Charles and Cowley, "An Early Source," 566. Cowley found his fragment among the Genizah materials at the Bodleian Library, Oxford.

[98]Ibid., 567-69.

[99]Ibid., 567.

[100]K[ohler], "Testaments of the Twelve Patriarchs," *The Jewish Encyclopedia* 12 (1906) 113-18.

[101] Alfred Bertholet, "Apokryphen und Pseudepigraphen," *Geschichte der althebräischen Litteratur* (ed. Karl Budde; Leipzig: C. F. Amelangs, 1906) 419-22.

[102]A. Schlatter, *Die Geschichte Israels von Alexander dem Grossen bis Hadrian* (2nd ed.; Stuttgart: Vereinsbuchhandlung, 1906) 250. The first edition (1901) offered the same opinion.

[103]Israel Lévi, "Notes sur le texte araméen du Testament de Lévi récemment découvert," *Revue des études juives* 54 (1907) 166-80; 55 (1908) 285-87.

[104]Robert Henry Charles (ed.), *The Greek Versions of the Testaments of the Twelve Patriarchs* (Oxford: Clarendon, 1908).

[105]R. H. Charles (ed.), *The Testaments of the Twelve Patriarchs, Translated from the Editor's Greek Text* (London: Adam and Charles Black, 1908).

[106]R. H. Charles (ed.), *The Apocrypha and Pseudepigrapha of the Old Testament* (2 vols.; Oxford: Clarendon, 1913).

[107]Charles (ed.), *The Testaments of the Twelve Patriarchs, Translated from the Editor's Greek Text* xviii-xxv.

[108]Ibid., xxv-xxvi.

[109]Ibid., xxvi.

[110]Ibid., xxvi-xxvii.

[111]Ibid., xxx-xxxii. The material on the Slavonic Version was prepared by W. R. Morfill.

[112]Ibid., xxxii-xxxv.

[113]Ibid., xlii.

[114]Ibid., xliii-xlvii. See p. 23 of this study.

[115]Ibid., xlvii-xlix.

[116]Ibid., l-liii.

[117]Ibid., lvii-lix.

[118]Ibid., lxxv.

[119]Ibid., lxxv-xcii.

[120]Ibid., xcii-xcv. See T Gad 6:3-7.

[121]R. H. Charles, "Man's Forgiveness of His Neighbor: A Study in Religious Development," *The Expositor*, 7th ser. 6 (1908) 492-505.

[122]Charles (ed.), *The Testaments of the Twelve Patriarchs, Translated from the Editor's Greek Text* xcii.

[123]Ibid., xcv. See T Iss 5:2, for example.

[124]Ibid., xcvi-xcvii.

CHAPTER IV

The Testaments of the Twelve Patriarchs and the Period 1908-1951: The Charles Consensus

J. E. Grabe had suggested in 1698 that the Testaments of the Twelve Patriarchs was a Jewish writing interpolated by a Christian. He was, however, a lone voice because every scholar who subsequently wrote on the Testaments from 1700 until 1884 asserted or assumed that the Testaments was an originally Christian writing. The only questions raised were those of date, place, type of Christian authorship, and interpolations. Between the appearance of F. Schnapp's work in 1884 and R. H. Charles' extensive introductions of 1908 the new consensus had been reached that the Testaments was, as Grabe had said, an originally Jewish writing with Christian interpolations.

The next period which we shall discuss covers the time from the publication of Charles' introductions until 1951. Research of this period is marked by two major characteristics. First, with rare exception it assumes that the Testaments is a Jewish document, and concerns itself primarily with questions of date, place, type of Jewish authorship, and with interpolations within the consensus established between 1884 and 1908. Second, this period ends with the new discussions of the Testaments in relationship to the finds at Qumran.

That the period 1908-1951 was controlled by the work of Charles becomes immediately clear in three discussions of the Testaments which appeared subsequent to his writings of 1908 but also in that year. F. Perles[1] noted that Charles had allowed scholars for the first time to see the Testaments with all of its Christian interpolations.[2] Perles then establishes the best Greek text by using the assumed Hebrew language original lying behind the present Greek.[3]

In the same year, A. Plummer[4] indicated the import of the ninety parallels between the Testaments and the NT given by Charles.[5] It is Plummer's object, however, to take issue with Charles' conclusion that the NT used the Testaments extensively.[6] According to Plummer there are twice as many parallels between Matthew and the Testaments as between all other Gospels together and the Testaments. He argues, therefore, that if Jesus had used the

Testaments, as Charles indicates in his introduction, the parallels would be found equally in all of the Gospels.[7] Since they are not, the conclusion is clear that it was the Testaments which used Matthew and not Jesus who used the Testaments.[8] Moreover, because the Testaments was originally written in Hebrew, the materials in the Testaments from Matthew must be later interpolations.[9] Finally, since Jesus did not use the Testaments and since Charles' evidence of a ca. 100 B.C.E. date of writing is not definitive, the Testaments may be dated between 100 B.C.E. and 50 C.E. It was translated into Greek ca. 100 C.E. with Christian interpolations added thereafter.[10]

In 1908-09 F. C. Burkitt, in his review[11] of Charles' work, offers a positive response to the evidence for the origin, date, and interpolations of the Testaments. On two important points, however, Burkitt disagrees with Charles. First, it cannot be shown that there are two separate Hebrew recensions because the same Christian interpolations appear in both of the supposed recensions.[12] Second, Charles' preference for many readings from Greek Group A is an error because Group A clearly alters the Group B text and is, therefore, later and inferior to it.[13]

Thus, in the same year as the publication of Charles' introduction and text of the Testaments, the mood of acceptance is set for the next four decades. Perles, Plummer, and Burkitt did have criticisms and alterations to make in the conclusions reached by Charles, but all three affirmed as conclusive his view that the Testaments is a Jewish writing with later interpolations.

Also in 1912 R. Leszynsky[14] accepted Charles' basic position concerning the origin of the Testaments, but at one interesting point reversed Charles' conclusions. Whereas Charles said that the original Hebrew document was written by a pro-Maccabean Pharisee who praised the levitical line, Leszynsky argues that it is more likely that a pro-Maccabean writer would be a Sadducee.[15] Moreover, T Naph 3:2 expresses a purely Sadducean attitude toward the Law.[16] Leszynsky does agree with Charles, however, that the Testaments contains Jewish interpolated materials against Levi and the Maccabees, written by a Pharisee opposed to the corrupt, later Maccabean line.[17] According to Leszynsky, therefore, the Testaments was originally a Sadducean document. Nonetheless, in its present form, it is a prime witness to the bitter war fought between Sadducees and Pharisees in the later Hasmonean period.[18]

Although S. Székely[19] offered a Charles-oriented summary of research in 1913 and Burkitt[20] repeated in 1914 his earlier position, the next significant discussions of the Testaments were those of J. W. Hunkin[21] and N. Messel.[22] Both had definite contributions to make toward Testaments research. Because in attacking Charles' text of the Testaments they also were attacking the very heart of his theories, it might appear that Hunkin and Messel serve as signs of the break up of the Charles consensus. This appearance is, however, misleading; no attention was paid to either of these men until after the end of the present period.

J. W. Hunkin makes a major attack upon the whole of Charles' text-critical formulation, using in part some of the criticisms already made by F. C. Burkitt.[23] According to Hunkin, Greek Group B is consistently superior to Group A;[24] this is shown on the basis of a comparison of verbal differences,[25] additions,[26] omissions,[27] and word order[28] in the two groups. Again, and for similar reasons, Armenian Group β is superior to Group α.[29] Most important, the Greek B and the Armenian β groups have very much in common.[30] For these reasons Hunkin concludes that the best critical text of the Testaments would be produced by using Greek Group B and Armenian Group β,[31] with the omissions of the Greek Group A and Armenian Group α in an apparatus. His final point is that Charles has not established the existence of the two Hebrew recensions.[32] It was not Hunkin's purpose in this article to reject Charles' theory that the Testaments is an originally Jewish document. He did reject, however, Charles' "scissors and paste method" of removing Christian materials from the Testaments[33] and showed that the longer, "Christian" text is the more original.[34]

But if Hunkin's text-critical study was only an implicit attack upon the Jewish origin theory proposed by Charles and his predecessors, this was not true of the largely text-critical study produced three years later by N. Messel. This scholar was convinced that the longer text (Armenian and Greek) was original and also Christian. First, Messel argues that the text preferred by Charles, with its omission of Christian material, shows a Judaism attested nowhere else, a Judaism with Christian teachings on universalism, neighbor-love, and the like.[35] Second, this same text with its eschatological destruction of the Jews could only have been written by a Christian.[36] Third, turning to text-critical arguments Messel discusses what Hunkin had called the "scissors and paste method" of Charles/Bousset, asking how these men could simply bracket and omit as interpolation Christian material still present in the Armenian Version.[37] Fourth, he asserts with Hunkin that Armenian Group α is a paraphrase of Group β; it may not be used to detect Christian interpolations.[38] Fifth, of the 220 sentences omitted by the Armenian Version, only thirty-one are specifically Christian.[39] Finally, on the basis of this last observation Messel concludes that the Armenian Version provides no means of discovering supposed Christian interpolations.[40]

Nonetheless, as noted above, these text-critical studies of Hunkin and Messel fell upon deaf ears for the next four decades, until they were finally brought to light by M. de Jonge in 1953. From 1908 until the 1950s, with the exception of Hunkin and Messel,[41] every study of the Testaments assumed the correctness of Charles' theory in its major thesis of a Jewish origin for the Testaments, and altered Charles either in some detail or discussed the Testaments on theological, sociological, or historical grounds within Charles' framework. We have seen this already in those scholars who wrote between 1908 and 1914 and we may now show the same movement between 1921 and 1951.

E. Meyer agreed with Charles that the Testaments was originally pro-levitical, and later interpolated by someone opposing the priesthood.[42] In opposition to Charles, however, Meyer argues that the original Testaments was written ca. 220 B.C.E.; the anti-Levi interpolations were added during the time of Jason and Menelaus, ca. 150 B.C.E.[43] In addition, Meyer notes that the Teacher in the Damascus Document from the Cairo Genizah and the Renewer of the Law in T Levi seem similar.[44] After the Qumran discoveries this observation will be elaborated greatly by A. Dupont-Sommer and his student, M. Philonenko.

In 1923 M. Dibelius described briefly the close parallels in the concept of spirit found in the Testaments, Shepherd of Hermas, and Persian dualism.[45] In 1927 V. Aptowitzer took up the Levi-Judah theme in the Testaments.[46] Whereas Ginzberg had insisted that the levitical Messiah could be paralleled only in the Epistle to the Hebrews, Aptowitzer argued that it must have been added to the Testaments by a Jewish interpolator because a Christian would not have stressed the levitical Messiah. He dismissed without any reference Ginzberg's mention of Hebrews.

In 1928[47] A. Causse[48] made an interesting social study of the Testaments in an attempt to discover its original *Sitz im Leben*. The key to this is T Issachar. Here the simple, honest life of the agricultural worker is portrayed;[49] and such a portrayal indicates that the Testaments was written in a rural setting.[50] Who were the writers? Bertholet was correct in his view that the hortatory materials in the Testaments derived from the simple, non-scribal, synagogue homily. Thus, the Testaments serves as a witness to the piety of the Ebionites, i. e., the honest, hard-working, rural Jews, who did not approve of nor participate in the wicked city life.[51]

Two years later R. Eppel affirmed almost entirely the position taken by Causse, seeing in the Testaments an excellent witness to the Jewish milieu of the NT.[52] More important, while he agrees with Charles in the question of language,[53] he makes two observations which run counter to Charles' position: first, he notes that in at least two places the Testaments uses the LXX;[54] second, he indicates that elsewhere an Aramaic original text appears present.[55] Eppel does not, however, follow these observations to any conclusion. Again, and here directly against Charles, he dates the Testaments with Meyer, arguing that the levitical role was of the greatest import not only after the beginning of the Maccabean period, but also immediately following the exile.[56] In the remainder of his study Eppel discusses the major theological motifs present in the Testaments as witness to the theology of rural Palestine near the end of the third century B.C.E.

M.-J. Lagrange had mentioned the Testaments briefly in 1909,[57] but had more to say in 1931.[58] According to him the theme of the Testaments is its moral exhortation, typical of certain segments of the Pharisaic community.[59] Not typical of Pharisaic exhortation, however, is the universalism and concern for the Gentiles found in the Testaments. Lagrange considers these to be Christian interpolations. They are not, as Charles has said, a new plateau in Jewish thought.[60]

But Lagrange's major concern in 1931 is not the question of the ethics of the Testaments. He is interested rather in the conception of messiahship and particularly in Charles' assertion that the Maccabean-Levite John Hyrcanus had assumed the royal messianic role previously held only by the tribe of Judah.[61] Lagrange agrees with Charles that it is the tribe of Levi which has prominence in the Testaments.[62] Moreover, he ascribes a place to Judah in our document only upon the basis of Judah's customary role as the embodiment of Israel.[63] The important question, however, is whether or not Charles was correct to see within the Testaments the passing of the messianic rights from the tribe of Judah to a specific person within another tribe, i.e., to John Hyrcanus within the tribe of Levi. To answer this question Lagrange discusses two texts, T Reuben 6:8-12 and T Levi 18:1-14.[64]

In the former text he finds that messianic terminology is used in reference to the tribe of Levi, but also that this terminology is without reference to any one Hasmonean.[65] In the latter text, where Charles had seen John Hyrcanus, Lagrange finds the whole early part of the Hasmonean line. Although he admits in these verses an apparent messianic reference to the levitical line, he understands this as hyperbole. Why? First, no Jew would change the traditional messianic line from one family to another. Second, messianic terminology was used regularly for those in power regardless of their claim to the genuine messianic line through Judah.[66]

R. T. Herford, two years later,[67] was not concerned primarily with the question of messiahship in the Testaments, although he agreed with Charles that John Hyrcanus is a central contemporary figure within the document.[68] In this he rejects the dating proposed by Meyer and Eppel and affirms that of Charles and Lagrange. With Bertholet, Lagrange, Causse, and Eppel he asserts that moral exhortation is the focal point of the Testaments.[69] But the author was not a Pharisee: first, Pharisees did not write down their teaching; second, Haggadah and Halakah, the major forms used by the Pharisees, are unimportant in the Testaments.[70]

Herford's most specific discussion deals with the God-neighbor love command and the universalism of the Testaments. Concerning the former, he says that the Testaments unites for the first time the OT commands of love toward God (Deut 6:5) and neighbor (Lev 19:18).[71] Concerning the latter, he notes that a universal outlook is not common in other Jewish writings of the period.[72] Neither of these motifs is, however, a Christian interpolation. Rather, the teachings of Jesus, which include these, originated in a type of Judaism reflected in the Testaments.[73]

Between 1945 and 1951 various discussions of the Testaments appeared; these conclude the description of the present period and show that to its end Charles was in control of Testaments study.

C. C. Torrey[74] disagrees with Charles only in dating the Testaments during the first century C.E. Ethelbert Stauffer,[75] in indicating similarities between the Johannine writings and the Testaments, argues that the Johannine materials come from the same Palestinian levitical circles as do the Testaments. Then in 1947 two articles appeared concerning T Levi 8. T. W. Manson[76] finds in T Levi 8:4-10 an early Syriac Christian rite of initiation. According to him, therefore, these verses are a Christian interpolation in the Jewish document;[77] consequently, the real beginning of the history of the tribe of Levi is at T Levi 8:11.[78] Therefore, in T Levi 8:14 it is not the Maccabees who are referred to but the Zadokites of Solomon prior to the Maccabees. Thus, Charles is wrong to see here a reference to the Maccabean priesthood.[79]

G. R. Beasley-Murray[80] immediately takes up Manson's observations and, noting in T Levi 8:11-15 the role of Judah as well as of Levi, concludes that the levitical Messiah has no exclusive prominence in the Testaments.[81] This leads him to insist further that the Levi-Judah pattern belongs to the original document, this against Charles who said the Judah messiahship was a later Jewish interpolation.[82]

Then, Matthew Black[83] argues that if T Levi 18 is not Christian, T Levi 18:6 ("as from Abraham to Isaac") is a messianic reference using Gen 22:8.[84] Because the theme of Gen 22:8 is the sacrifice of Isaac, Black concludes that

there can be no doubt that the voice of the Father to His Messiah in Levi 18, a voice like Abraham's to Isaac, is the voice of parental authority calling for the obedience of a beloved Son to the point of complete readiness to offer Himself in Sacrifice.

According to Black, therefore, Isa 53:7 stands behind T Levi 18:6, and T Levi 18:6 itself is the basis for the Christian theme of the sacrifice of God's Son.

J. R. Porter[85] immediately rejected Black's analysis. Porter first indicates that the reading "as from Abraham to Isaac" is questionable because a significant part of the MSS read "as from Abraham the Father of Jacob." This latter reading removes any reference to Gen 22:8. Second, and granted the superiority of Black's reading, Porter argues that the context of T Levi 18:6 is not sacrifice but sanctification. Furthermore, while in the OT Abraham speaks to Isaac only in Genesis 22:8, Jub 21:1-25 has a long blessing of Isaac by Abraham; here again the theme is sanctification and not sacrifice. Porter's conclusion: T Levi 18:6 does not speak of messianic suffering; it does not serve, therefore, as a bridge between Isaiah's Suffering Servant and the sacrificial Messiah of Christianity.

In 1950 E. J. Bickerman and A. Lods again make clear our assertion that the period from 1908 until the introduction of the Qumran materials is firmly governed by R. H. Charles' work. While Lods[86] simply recapitulates the position of Charles in 1908, Bickerman[87] on the other hand affirms the basic position of Charles concerning the Jewish origin and Christian interpolation of the Testaments, but disagrees with him about the nature of some of these interpolations and about the date of the original document.

Bickerman agrees with Meyer that the original Testaments was written between 200 and 175 B.C.E., because of numismatic evidence from T Jos 16:4-5. The coins referred to in these verses were in use before 285 B.C.E. and shortly after 200 B.C.E. Because a pre-285 B.C.E. date of writing appears to be too early, one subsequent to 200 B.C.E. is to be preferred. Additional evidence for such a date is provided by T Naph 5:8, which refers to contemporary Seleucid rule. Further, contrary to Charles, T Reuben 6:5-12 may not be used to date the Jewish Testaments because it is a Christian interpolation. Thus, Charles' view is wrong that John Hyrcanus was the priestly Messiah of the Testaments.[88] Finally, on one other important point Bickerman disputes Charles. The latter had said that the anti-Levi materials in the Testaments were interpolated since much of the Testaments is strongly pro-Levi. According to Bickerman, however, this apparent literary contradiction is not a sign of interpolation; it is entirely in keeping with the original document which, for each of the tribes, speaks of a future disobedience and condemnation.[89]

While Lods and Bickerman show the continued centrality of Charles in the period under discussion, this is even more so with the final article to be mentioned in this chapter. As its title indicates, A. W. Argyle's study[90] assumes the Jewish origin of the Testaments. Similar to Charles' various lists of Testaments-NT parallels, it takes for granted that these parallels are in fact dependencies of the NT upon the Testaments. Argyle's first four parallels show that the Gospels consciously ascribe the qualities of Joseph to Jesus. Specifically, Joseph and Jesus are delivered up out of envy (T Gad 6:3,7 / Matt 18:15,35; Mark 15:15); both are "innocent blood" sold for silver (T Zeb 2:2 / Matt 27:4); both are hungry, alone, sick, and in prison (T Jos 1:5b-7 / Matt 25:35); neither is haughty (T Jos 17:8-18:1 / Luke 22:27; Luke 14:11; Matt 18:4; Matt 23:12). Argyle's other parallels are more general and without the Joseph-Jesus typology; since they show the use of the Testaments in Acts and Paul, however, Argyle concludes that this document was used frequently in the whole NT.

Our description of the period from the publication of Charles' introductions and text of the Testaments to just before the addition of the Qumran evidence to the discussion shows how completely the position of Charles dominated the study of the Testaments of the Twelve Patriarchs. It was this situation which precluded a hearing for the significant studies of Hunkin and Messel in the middle of the period. Of course there were disagreements with Charles in questions of authorship, date, and interpolations; but no one with the exception of Hunkin and Messel offered any criticism of his basic literary-, source-, and text-critical suppositions or of his basic schema of a Hebrew original document with later interpolations. In the case of Burkitt and Herford, where such criticisms were made, these were not allowed to alter the fundamental Charles position.

Moreover, while the 1950s and 1960s will offer new evidence and some different theories about the origins of the document, it will still be true that the contributions of the 18th and 19th centuries remain forgotten. Charles had won the day. His position had obliterated the past; the long period from 1908 to 1950 assumed his work as conclusive, and even the new researches of the past twenty years have not dimmed its prominence.

FOOTNOTES

[1]Felix Perles, "Zur Erklärung der Testamente der zwölf Patriarchen," *Beihefte zur Orientalischen Litteraturzeitung* [2] (1908) 10-18.

[2]Ibid., 10.

[3]Ibid., 11-18.

[4]Alfred Plummer, "The Relations of the Testaments of the Twelve Patriarchs to the Books of the New Testament," *The Expositor*, 7th ser. 6 (1908) 481-91.

[5]Ibid., 481.

[6]Ibid., 482.

[7]Ibid., 484.

[8]Ibid., 485.

[9]Ibid., 486.

[10]Ibid., 486-90.

[11]F. C. Burkitt, rev. of R. H. Charles (ed.), *The Greek Versions of the Testaments of the Twelve Patriarchs*, JTS 10 (1908) 135-41.

[12]Ibid., 137.

[13]Ibid., 138-39.

[14]Rudolf Leszynsky, *Die Sadduzäer* (Berlin: Mayer und Müller, 1912) 237-52.

[15]Ibid., 237. According to Louis Ginzberg, who wrote two years later ("Eine unbekannte jüdische Sekte," *Monatsschrift für Geschichte und Wissenschaft des Judentums* 58 [1914] 404-09), it is not clear that the Jewish writer of the Testaments was pro-levitical. After analysis of T Reuben 6:7-12 and T Levi 8:14 Ginzberg concluded that no reference to a priestly Messiah could be found in these texts. The reference is rather to a Messiah from Judah. The appearance of a priestly Messiah in the Testaments is to be explained simply as a Christian interpolation based on Hebrews.

[16]Leszynsky, *Die Sadduzäer* 250.

[17]Ibid., 238-39.

[18]Ibid., 242-43.

[19]Stephan Székely, *Bibliotheca apocrypha: Introductio historico-critica in libros apocryphos utriusque Testamenti cum explicatione argumenti et doctrinae* (Freiburg: B. Herder, 1913) 382-422.

[20]F. Crawford Burkitt, *Jewish and Christian Apocalypses* (London: H. Milford, 1914) 34-36.

[21]J. W. Hunkin, "The Testaments of the Twelve Patriarchs," *JTS* 16 (1914) 80-97.

[22]N. Messel, "Über die textkritisch begründete Ausscheidung vermutlicher christlicher Interpolationen in den Testamenten der zwölf Patriarchen," BZAW 33 (1918) 355-74.

[23]Hunkin, "The Testaments," 80.

[24]Ibid., 81.

[25]Ibid., 87.

[26]Ibid., 83-87.

[27]Ibid., 87-89.

[28]Ibid., 89.

[29]Ibid., 95.

[30]Ibid., 95-96.

[31]Ibid., 96.

[32]Ibid.

[33]M.-J.Lagrange (*Le messianisme chez les juifs* [Paris: Victor Lecoffre, 1909] 68) had already questioned Charles' right to remove references to Jesus while allowing references very close to Jesus' teaching to remain.

[34]Hunkin, "The Testaments," 96.

[35]Messel, "Über die textkritisch begründete Ausscheidung vermutlicher christlicher Interpolationen," 356.

[36]Ibid., 357.

[37]Ibid., 357-59.

[38]Ibid., 364.

[39]Ibid., 373.

[40]Ibid., 374.

[41]Gustav Karpeles (*Geschichte der jüdischen Literatur* [4th ed., unchanged from 3rd ed. of 1920; Graz: Akademischer Druck, 1963] 1. 159) said the Testaments may be either a Jewish or a Christian writing, but offered no defense of this position.

[42]Ed. Meyer, *Ursprung und Anfänge des Christentums* (Berlin: J. G. Cotta, 1921) 2. 168.

[43]Ibid.

[44]Ibid., 172.

[45]Martin Dibelius, *Der Hirt des Hermas* (Tübingen: J. C. B. Mohr, 1923) 517-19. P. A. Munch ("The Spirit in the Testaments of the Twelve Patriarchs," *AcOr* 13 [1935] 257-63) will argue that the spirits in the Testaments are of two kinds, the genuine demonic/angelic and the psychological. He believes the former were interpolated since they appear primarily in the apocalyptic sections of the Testaments considered by Schnapp to be interpolations.

[46]V. Aptowitzer, *Parteipolitik der Hasmonäerzeit im rabbinischen und pseudepigraphischen Schrifttum* (Vienna: Kohut Foundation, 1927) 88-90.

[47]It should be noted that in 1927 M. R. James ("The Venice Abstract from the Testaments of the Twelve Patriarchs." *JTS* 28 [1927] 337-48) offered an additional Greek text of parts of the Testaments.

[48]A. Causse, "L'ideal ébionitique dans les Testaments des douze patriarches," *Congrès d'histoire du christianisme* (ed. P. L. Couchoud; Paris: Rieder, 1928) 1. 55-76.

[49]Ibid., 56-61.

[50]Ibid., 60.

[51]Ibid., 59-61, 67.

[52]Robert Eppel, *Le piétisme juif dans les Testaments des douze patriarches* (Paris: Félix Alcan, 1930) viii.

[53]Ibid., 14.

[54]Ibid.

[55]Ibid., 16-17.

[56]Ibid., 30-32.

[57]Lagrange, *Le messianisme* 68.

[58]M.-J. Lagrange, *Le judaïsme avant Jésus-Christ* (Paris: Librarie Lecoffre, 1931) 122-30.

[59]Ibid., 122-23, 130.

[60]Ibid., 122-23.

[61]Ibid., 124-29.

[62]Ibid., 125.

[63]Ibid.

[64]Ibid., 126.

[65]Ibid.

[66]Ibid., 127-29.

[67]R. Travers Herford, *Talmud and Apocrypha, a Comparative Study of the Jewish Ethical Teaching in the Rabbinical and Non-Rabbinical Sources in the Early Centuries* (London: Soncino, 1933) 233-43.

[68]Ibid., 233.

[69]Ibid.

[70]Ibid., 237, 191-94.

[71]Ibid., 238-39.

[72]Ibid., 240.

[73]Similarly, J. Bonsirven (*Le Judaïsme palestinien au temps de Jésus-Christ* [Paris: Gabriel Beauchesne et ses fils, 1934] 2. 294) said that the ethics of the Testaments are higher than those of the other post-Biblical Jewish writings. Also, G. G. Fox ("Testaments of the Twelve Patriarchs," *The Universal Jewish Encyclopedia* 10[1943] 202) affirmed ten years later Herford's view that the two-fold love command in the Testaments was the source of Jesus' teaching.

[74]Charles Cutler Torrey, *The Apocryphal Literature, a Brief Introduction* (New Haven: Yale, 1945) 129-31.

[75]Ethelbert Stauffer, *Die Theologie des Neuen Testaments* (Geneva: Oikumene Verlag, 1945) 318-21.

[76]T. W. Manson, "Testaments of the XII Patr.: Levi VIII," *JTS* 48 (1947) 59-61.

[77]Ibid., 59-60.

[78]Ibid., 61.

[79]Ibid.

[80]G. R. Beasley-Murray, "The Two Messiahs in the Testaments of the Twelve Patriarchs," *JTS* 48 (1947) 1-12.

[81]Ibid., 5.

[82]Ibid., 5, 11. Aptowitzer saw the Levi-Judah material as a Jewish interpolation. L. Mariès ("Le messie issu de Lévi chez Hippolyte de Rome," *RevScRel* 39 [1951] 381-96) will see the Testaments as Hyppolytus' source for the two Messiahs.

[83]Matthew Black, "The Messiah in the Testament of Levi *XVIII*," *ExpT* 60 (1948-1949) 321-22.

[84]T Levi 18.6 refers here to Gen 22:8 because in this OT verse alone does Abraham speak to Isaac.

[85]J. R. Porter, "The Messiah in the Testament of Levi XVIII," *ExpT* 61 (1949-1950) 90-91.

[86]Adolfe Lods, *Histoire de la littérature hébräique et juive depuis les origines jusqu'à la ruine de l'état juif* (Paris: Payot, 1952) 818-24.

[87]Elias J. Bickerman, "The Date of the Testaments of the Twelve Patriarchs," *JBL* 69 (1950) 245-60.

[88]Ibid., 251, 260.

[89]Ibid., 249.

[90]A. W. Argyle, "The Influence of the Testaments of the Twelve Patriarchs upon the New Testament," *ExpT* 63 (1951-1952) 256-58.

CHAPTER V

1952-1958: Qumran or Christian Origins for the Testaments? The Discussion Begun

It had been my intention in the next two chapters to deviate from the chronological presentation in order to turn, for the sake of clarity, to a more topically oriented description because the materials from 1952 to the present have three foci — the Testaments in relationship to Qumran, to early Christianity, and to non-sectarian Judaism. Nonetheless, a chronological presentation of the period is, I believe, necessary. First, the diversity of research from 1952 to the present should be shown without schematic distortion. Second, and more important, the three foci of the period are constantly interwoven and mutually enriched so as to make any topical presentation a rending, so to speak, of the fabric.

The object of the next two chapters is to show relationships and developing lines. For the moment, however, it may be of value to the reader to have some pegs on which to hang the elements of the discussion. These pegs (corresponding to the three foci previously mentioned) will also serve as a useful overview to the period. The first of these is Qumran. Beginning in 1952 the finds from Qumran have induced scholars to offer various theories about the origins of the Testaments at Qumran. The second peg is the renewal of interest in the possibility of a Christian origin for the Testaments; the third is the return to the position of Charles, or one similar to it, which sees the Testaments as a product of non-sectarian Judaism. In general, theories advocating a Qumranian or Christian origin have dominated the last twenty years of discussion and the position associated with Charles has been secondary. It is true, however, that the Qumran theories are but a modification of Charles since both place the Testaments in the milieu of intertestamental Judaism. A scholar such as J. Becker simply carries Charles' methods and theory of origins to its logical conclusion. It may suffice to say that in the period about to be discussed there was wide and constant interplay among theories of Qumranian, Christian, and non-sectarian Jewish origins for the Testaments.

The Possibility of Qumranian Origin

Already in 1921 E. Meyer[1] had noted the similarity between the Teacher of the Damascus Document in the Cairo Genizah finds and the priest in the Testaments who would renew the Law. C. Rabin was the first to take up this issue in the present period when, in 1952, he noted the similarities between the Teacher in the Damascus Document and the Unique Prophet in T Benj 9:2. Rabin's point is that, since no Christian would speak of a "unique prophet," this text probably comes from Qumran, either originally or as an interpolation.[2]

Also in 1952, J. P. Audet attempted to show that the Two Ways of Christian literature arose at Qumran as attested by 1 QS 3:13 — 4:26. In this article Audet appears to assume the Qumranian origin of the Testaments.[3] So also in its continuation in 1953[4] he makes the same assumption, but here it becomes clearer that it is based upon at least two grounds, i.e., the presence of the Two Ways and Two Angels in the Qumran literature and in the Testaments.[5]

But the articles by Rabin, Audet, and Kuhn (see note 5) which indicate close historical and theological parallels between the Testaments and the Qumran literature, are preliminary in that they do not work in a systematic fashion with the constellation of relationships between the Testaments and the Qumran writings. The same may not be said, however, of the work of two other scholars who discussed these relationships in 1953. A. Dupont-Sommer was the first to argue an extended case for the presence of the Teacher from Qumran in the Testaments; and B. Otzen was the first to gather into a whole the theological parallels between the Testaments and Qumran.

According to A. Dupont-Sommer[6] the Testaments was written at Qumran. Just as fragments of Enoch and Jubilees have been found there, so also will Testaments fragments yet be found.[7] By using the Habakkuk Commentary from Qumran and T Levi, a history of events in the Qumran Community can be established in the following way.[8] T Levi 17 concerns the good and bad Hasmonean priesthood. The first priest mentioned is Judas and the fourth is John Hyrcanus. After John Hyrcanus come the bad priests. T Levi 10, 14, 15, 16 also describe the good priests and their persecution by the bad.[9] Now, since the Habakkuk Commentary also speaks of this persecution, Dupont-Sommer concludes that the Teacher of Qumran must be one of the good priests in the Testaments.[10] And in T Levi 18, where eschatological times are described, a new priest arises who is clearly the Teacher of Qumran. This figure dies but rules eschatologically; he is, therefore, the messianized Teacher.[11] Indeed, T Levi 18 provides the first instance of the Qumran Teacher's messianization.[12]

Thus, Dupont-Sommer looked quite differently upon the messianic passage T Levi 18. Scholars who defended the Christian origin of the Testaments used this chapter to prove that the Christian Messiah is central to the Testaments. Scholars who had defended a Jewish origin tended to see it as a Christian interpolation; but according to Dupont-Sommer it is neither Christian nor interpolated. On the contrary, it belongs to the original document and refers to the messianic Teacher at Qumran. Therefore, the Testaments is a product of Qumran useful in the historical reconstruction of that community.

B. Otzen's extensive article of 1953 on the relationship between Qumran and the Testaments might seem to confirm the Qumran origin of the Testaments.[13] However, at least in terms of Dupont-Sommer's conclusions, it does not:

> Es lässt sich nicht behaupten, dass Test XII. und die neuen Schriften aus derselben Sekte herrühren, denselben historischen Hintergrund haben und dieselben historischen Ereignisse widerspiegeln.[14]

In spite of this conclusion, Otzen does find important parallels between the Testaments and Qumran in four areas: ethics, dualistic theology, demonology/angelology, and messiology. Under the first of these, Otzen shows that the ethic of the Damascus Document is Pharisaic and unlike the Manual of Discipline which is more typical of Qumran. He gives examples to show that the Manual and the Testaments have a similar ethic stressing Torah-piety and love of neighbor.[15]

Under the second area, dualistic theology, Otzen again distinguishes the Damascus Document from the Manual of Discipline. Although the Testaments and the latter have a similar ethical-psychological dualism, they differ in that the Manual also offers a mythological dualism between good and evil.[16] Then, concerning demonology/angelology, he indicates the similar role of Beliar in the Testaments and the Qumran literature.[17]

Under the fourth area he first questions the validity of Dupont-Sommer's views about the Teacher from Qumran in T Levi 18.[18] In order to deal with this issue, Otzen discusses four questions. First, does T Levi 17 speak of the seven Hasmonean rulers? Probably not; rather it concerns the whole Aaronic priesthood.[19] Second, how valuable are T Levi 10, 14, 16, 17 for Dupont-Sommer's argument? According to Otzen there is nothing in these sections clearly about the Teacher. T Levi 10:2 and T Levi 14:2 refer to Jesus; T Levi 16:3 and T Levi 17 are general historical references about the priesthood.[20] Third, what evidence is there in the Qumran literature that the Teacher was murdered? There is none.[21] Fourth, is the Teacher a messianic feature in the Damascus Document or Habakkuk Commentary? He is not; CD 6:10 does not concern his return at the last day, but Elijah's.[22]

Finally, Otzen examines the question of the doctrine of two Messiahs at Qumran and in the Testaments, concluding that both teach such a doctrine.[23] With this he reaches his main conclusion: while the Testaments and Qumran exhibit many theological parallels, they do not exhibit the historical parallels asserted by Dupont-Sommer.[24]

Thus, already in 1953 the Qumran materials had begun to make a major contribution to the research on the question of the origin of the Testaments.

Dupont-Sommer was sure that the key historical link was the Teacher from Qumran and that eventually the Testaments itself would be found among the MSS of Qumran. Otzen was impressed with the many theological parallels but not at all with the historical parallels and dependencies. It will be difficult from now on to study the Testaments without keeping in mind its affinities to the Qumran literature.

The Renewed Possibility of Christian Origin

The year 1953 was not over; if Qumran was going to have a major influence on the future of Testaments research, so too was M. de Jonge's study published in the same year.[25] De Jonge pays little attention to the Qumran materials.[26] It is his intention to show rather that the Testaments is a Christian compilation. And in so doing he becomes the first scholar in seventy years (with the exception of Messel) to defend the pre-1884 consensus of scholarship.

De Jonge begins his study by indicating that it is primarily the position of R. H. Charles which he intends to oppose;[27] he thus confirms the findings of our last chapter that Charles had lost none of his authority over the forty years since his publications in 1908. In Chapter 1 de Jonge discusses the manuscript witnesses to the Testaments in Greek, Slavonic, and Armenian in order to evaluate Charles' use of this evidence to remove Christian interpolations. Concerning the Greek MSS de Jonge concludes, with the help of Hunkin's article, that the Group A MSS are a free recension of the Group B MSS. Within Group B de Jonge finds two sub-groups, γ and δ, of which δ is to be preferred; MS b (Cambridge University Library MS Ff I.24) is the best witness in sub-group δ.[28] According to de Jonge the Slavonic Version is most closely related to sub-group γ.[29] Concerning the Armenian Version, he agrees with Charles both that it appears in Groups α and β, and that Group β is generally superior (vs. Preuschen) to Group α; this latter is a short redaction of β. In general, the Armenian Version is closest to Greek sub-group δ.[30]

De Jonge next examines the specific verses in the Testaments claimed by Charles and Bousset, on the basis of the Armenian Version, to be Christian interpolations.[31] He concludes that "A [Armenian Version] is of little value for the discovery and removal of Christian additions to the Greek text."[32] Using the same method[33] to evaluate the interpolations derived from the Greek text, he offers the following conclusion:

> Thus the examination of all cases where Bousset and Charles remove Christian interpolations on textual grounds, shows that only in a very few cases is it possible to assume such an interpolation. This is little enough ground for a general theory which would explain the co-existence of Christian and Jewish passages in the Testaments by assuming Christian interpolations into a Jewish original.[34]

Having now shown that the Christian materials in the Testaments are text-critically integral to it,[35] de Jonge goes on to describe the sources and methods used by the Christian compiler. To do this he first works with T Levi.

Comparison of the Jewish T Levi fragments[36] with parallels to the Testaments' T Levi leads him to conclude that the latter must have as its source a Jewish Original Levi.[37] De Jonge shows, however, that the author of the Testaments has altered his source so it would support his own particular Christian purposes and concerns.[38] Thus, the Christian interpolation theory is not correct. A Christian did not add materials to a Jewish writing; rather, a Christian author used a Jewish source in the preparation of his own compilation.[39]

Similarly, the Hebrew fragment of a T Naphtali[40] shows parallels with the T Naphtali of the Testaments.[41] These have a common source which de Jonge calls Original Naphtali.[42] The Christian compiler has changed his source, particularly in removing the anti-Joseph material from it.[43] Of major import, however, is the fact that Original Levi and Original Naphtali reveal little in common and do not appear to have been written as parts of the same document. Thus, de Jonge concludes that the Testaments of the Twelve Patriarchs as we know it is the first testamentary document gathering together all of the Patriarchs.[44]

De Jonge next discusses the haggadic materials in T Judah 3-19; he finds close parallels here with Midrash Wayissa'u. For the section T Judah 3-7 he concludes that the writer of the Testaments was dependent upon material like that contained in this Midrash; the Christian author has altered these, however, for his own purposes.[45] Again, the traditions in T Judah 9 are parallel to those of the Midrash and Jubilees;[46] and those of T Judah 8, 10-12, 13-19 are similar to what is contained in Jubilees.[47] This leads de Jonge to the view that the Testaments and Jubilees used common Hebrew tradition like that preserved in Midrash Wayissa'u:

> When our author had conceived his plan to compose Testaments of the Twelve Patriarchs, because he knew two Jewish Testaments of Levi and Naphtali, he looked for further material to illustrate the lives of the other patriarchs and found it in this haggadic source.[48]

De Jonge follows the above with a brief but important section on the Reuben-Bilhah episode (T Reuben 3:9). Here he shows that Jubilees and the Testaments tell the same story with different intentions.

> T Reuben uses it to warn against fornication and to emphasize the power of repentance, Jubilees XXXIII 9b-20 connects with this episode the law which forbids intercourse with one's father's wife and lays all emphasis on the fact that according to this law this sin must be punished with death.[49]

It is the Christian writer himself, therefore, who introduced the same strong note of ethical exhortation throughout T Reuben.[50]

In T Issachar, however, de Jonge finds little use of traditions other than those already in the LXX. This testament is composed by the writer of the Testaments without the restrictions produced by the use of sources. Therefore, because of the many similarities between T Issachar and the others, it is clear that one author has compiled the whole document.[51]

Having shown that the Christian compiler used Jewish sources for his own paraenetic purpose, de Jonge next discusses themes which run throughout the Testaments. Specifically, he deals with the Sin-Exile-Return (S.E.R.), Levi-Judah (L.J.), messianic, and Joseph passages. He says that the Sin-Exile-Return passages probably are drawn by the Christian compiler from Original Levi; however, they have been altered thoroughly by the compiler.[52] Similarly, the Levi-Judah pattern derives from Original Naphtali, where it served to make Israel obedient to Judah as king and to Levi as priest. A study of these passages reveals that in some instances the Christian writer has altered them while in others he has not.[53] De Jonge makes the following significant point about the altered texts:

> In these passages, with the exception of T. N. viii 2f., the author connects Christ with the tribe of Judah as well as with the tribe of Levi. This does not mean that he regards Christ as a descendant of Judah as well as of Levi. T.N. viii 2f., T. Jos. xix 8, and T.L. xviii, T. Jud. xxiv clearly refer to a Messiah from Judah alone. We must assume that the author, having both Levi and Judah before him in the L.J.-pattern, tried to resolve the difficulty by connecting Christ as high priest with the tribe of Levi and as king with the tribe of Judah.[54]

In his discussion of the messianic passages de Jonge deals particularly with T Levi 18 and T Judah 24. Both are hymns which glorify Christ.[55] Finally, in an analysis of the Joseph passages, de Jonge says that this figure is a prime example of virtue in the Testaments and the type of Christ preceded in importance only by Levi and Judah.[56] Moreover, in the materials on Joseph and Potiphar, de Jonge finds an additional source for the Christian writer, this probably an already Judaized hellenistic romance.[57]

The last section of Chapter 2 discusses the introduction and conclusion to each of the individual testaments. Because all of these are similar, de Jonge believes that the Testaments is the product of one man.[58]

Chapter 3 is a recapitulation of previous conclusions and an attempt to ascribe a date to the Testaments. On the basis of theological parallels between certain of the Church Fathers and the Testaments, de Jonge concludes that the period 190 to 225 C.E. is the time of composition.[59] Given this date, he then deals with the issue of the authorship of the Testaments. Because its christology is not precise, its author was "an ordinary Christian who was not very interested in the exactness of his dogmatic terminology."[60] This same lack of precision leads de Jonge to conclude that the writer was not involved in the Church's christological debates. Where did he write? We do not know; it is unlikely, however, that he wrote in Palestine because he takes no definite stand vis-à-vis the Jews and is not well informed about Palestinian geography.[61]

Early Responses to the New Proposals of Qumran and Christian Origins

In 1950 it was thought that the problem of the origin of the Testaments had been resolved. The Charles consensus had ruled for almost fifty years. But just as Schnapp in 1884 had ended abruptly the predominance of Jewish-Christian authorship theories, so in 1953 the consensus was again disrupted and this time from two directions. According to Dupont-Sommer, Qumran offered the answer to the riddle; and for de Jonge, orthodox Christian piety at the end of the second century was the key. Contention primarily between these two positions will take up the remainder of the 1950s.

While J. W. Doeve's review in 1954[62] had few criticisms of de Jonge, D. R. Jones[63] agreed only with the latter's text-critical analysis; otherwise he argued against him on three points. First, the existence of a Levi-Judah pattern, which in some instances lacked a Christian reference, indicates the pre-Christian origin of the Testaments; second, to find much of his Christian material de Jonge over-allegorized the text; third, if the Testaments appears at Qumran, it does not have a Christian origin.

Whereas B. Otzen had pointed out parallels between the Testaments and the Qumran documents without supposing a dependency of the former upon the latter, in 1955 K. G. Kuhn's article[64] concerning the doctrine of the two Messiahs faced the question of dependency with much greater boldness. After discussing this doctrine in the Manual of Discipline and the Testaments,[65] Kuhn concludes that Charles was wrong to have placed the Levi and Judah Messiahs in different strata of the Testaments.[66] Moreover, "dass die Test. XII von Haus aus in dem Kreis des essenischen Schrifttums gehören, zeigt ihre Sprache und Gedankenwelt auf Schritt und Tritt."[67]

Although P. H. Aschermann's dissertation[68] of the same year did not agree with Kuhn that the Testaments originated at Qumran, it certainly did agree with him in its rejection of de Jonge's theory. Already in the introduction to this first form-critical study of the Testaments, Aschermann gives three reasons why the document is not Christian in origin: first, the Armenian Version exhibits a less Christian text than the Greek MSS; second, one can show a second century Christian tendency to alter Jewish writings; and third, the Testaments appears to be among the documents found at Qumran.[69]

Aschermann's description of the four-fold form of each of the testaments (framework, life history, paraenesis, future sayings) leads him to conclude that the basic form used is the Old Testament farewell discourse (Abschiedsrede).[70] So too, the paraenesis of the Testaments has a four-fold form: introduction with imperative followed by ὅτι or γάρ; description of the particular vice or virtue; example; conclusion, usually with imperative.[71] Concerning the possible Christian origin of this paraenesis, Aschermann says that it is no more Christian than Ben Sirach or the Pirke Aboth.[72] Nonetheless, in a brief discussion of the future sayings, he does conclude that most of these are, in their present form, Christian.[73] The two-Messiah doctrine existed, however, in the Jewish Testaments and shows the document's origin within the period of John Hyrcanus.[74] The future sayings are in any case of secondary import when compared to the paraenesis of the Testaments.[75]

At this point Aschermann begins the central part of his dissertation, the description of the various forms of paraenesis within the Testaments.[76] The first of these is the "negative descriptive series" in which, as in T Iss 4:1-6, the evil deeds avoided by the good man are listed. This form appears throughout the Testaments and has close parallels in the Old Testament and contemporary Jewish writings, particularly in Ben Sirach.[77] Similarly, the "positive descriptive series" (T Gad 5:1, for example), with its enumeration of the results of particular vices, finds close parallels in Jewish Wisdom literature.[78] Then follows a discussion of the "conditional negative descriptive series" (T Gad 4:1-5, for example) with its parallels in Ben Sirach and other Wisdom literature[79] and the "confessions of guiltlessness" (T Zeb 1:4-5, for example) with parallels in the Psalms and Job.[80] Because this last form is cultic in the Psalms but not in Job or the Testaments, Aschermann concludes that the paraenesis of the Testaments is "late Jewish."[81] He then distinguishes the "praise poetry of salvation," "conditional wisdom-saying series," "imperative poems," and "antithetical sentences."[82] On the basis of his form analysis Aschermann draws the following conclusions: first, the paraenesis of the Testaments is Jewish in form; second, the Testaments itself is a literary work from the mainstream of "late" Judaism; and third, it was composed in the late second century B.C.E., because of parallels with Ben Sirach, Jubilees, and the Qumran literature.[83]

In the last part of his dissertation Aschermann deals with paraenetical forms present in the Testaments and in early Christianity.[84] According to his findings few Testaments forms appear either in early Christianity or the Judaism of the periods following the writing of our document.[85] Paul, in 1 Thes 2:1ff and 2 Cor 12:11ff, used a confession of guiltlessness[86] and in 1 Cor 13:4-7 a negative descriptive series,[87] while Acts 20:18-35 is a "Testament of Paul."[88] Otherwise, forms similar to those of the Testaments are found only in the Jewish materials of the Mandates of Hermas.[89] In the Mandates, however, they have been reworked by Christian hands. For this reason Aschermann asks de Jonge why the Testaments has no similar Christian reworking of the paraenesis.[90]

It is apparent, therefore, that the early responses to de Jonge's study were not positive. This soon changed, however, when two well-known scholars wrote favorably of his work and when, more important, the Qumran texts were brought to the defense of his position. R. M. Grant accepted de Jonge's literary analysis and questioned him only on his dating of the document. Because the same exegesis of the OT appears in the Testaments, Justin, Theophilus, the same thought world in the Testaments and Hermas, and because Syrian Christian pre-baptismal unction may be found in the Testaments, it must have been written "well before the end of the second century in Syria."[91] Also J. Daniélou was impressed with de Jonge's method and conclusions[92] but not with his dating nor author. In the opinion of Daniélou, the teaching on the seven heavens and the Christ-Michael identification date the Testaments near the end of the first century and suggest Jewish-Christian authorship.[93]

The most important defense of de Jonge came, however, from an unexpected quarter. Dupont-Sommer and Jones were right: a Testaments discovered at Qumran would prove that the present Testaments is not an original Christian composition. At this juncture, J. T. Milik[94] announced that a fragment of a testament of Levi in Aramaic (suggested date ca. 100 B. C. E.) had been found at Qumran.[95] While he does not discuss similarities and differences between this testament and the T Levi of the Testaments, he does insist that this find is *not* the proof which Dupont-Sommer and Jones were seeking. On the contrary, and this is important in light of the continuing misunderstanding of the issue,

> rappelons en fin que dans les lots de Qumrân il n'y a aucun reste d'un original sémitique des Test. XII Patr. Étant donné l'extrême richesse et la varieté de la trouvaille, ce fait exclut pratiquement l'origine prechrétienne et palestinienne de l'apocryphe. Et tout porte à croire que les Test. XII Patr. sont une composition judéo-chrétienne, utilisant largement les ouvrages juifs proprement dits....[96]

That is, the Aramaic T Levi fragment shows that the Testaments uses Jewish materials; de Jonge had also come to this conclusion. More important, the Qumran discoveries show that the Testaments is probably a Christian writing, because it is not among the large number of Jewish documents found at the Dead Sea. This last observation is particularly significant in terms of Dupont-Sommer's statement that the Testaments would appear at Qumran.

In the same volume Milik also reviewed de Jonge's book. Here too he is supportive of de Jonge's position,[97] while agreeing with Audet that the Testaments and Qumran have much in common.[98] Against de Jonge he notes that the Dan-Satan motif appears already in Revelation and the Temple veil motif in the "Life of the Prophets" from ca. 100 C. E. Therefore, he dates the Testaments at the end of the first century, suggesting that it is quite possibly a Palestinian Jewish-Christian writing.[99]

H. F. D. Sparks, however, was not so sure that de Jonge had made a strong case, since much of the content of the Testaments is not necessarily Christian.[100] On the other hand, he does say that de Jonge's text-critical evidence has weakened the Charles position; it will be difficult to use the Testaments as a Jewish document until the Jewish original is discovered.[101]

The remainder of 1955 and 1956 was taken up with three source-critical matters related to the Testaments. In two articles P. Grelot analyzes the various fragments of materials similar to T Levi which had appeared among the Cairo Genizah and Qumran finds. In the first article[102] he reconstructs the Aramaic text of Col. c 10 — d 1 using the Greek Mt. Athos fragment.[103] From this Grelot draws the following conclusions: first, the Greek is not dependent upon the Aramaic fragment; second, an Aramaic original does stand nonetheless behind the Greek fragment; third, both the Aramaic fragment and the Aramaic original behind the Greek fragment derive from the same Hebrew source.[104] In a second article[105] Grelot discusses the Aramaic T Levi in the Bodleian Col. a and its parallels in Jubilees 31 and T Levi 9. He finds that the

Bodleian fragment summarizes its parallel in Jubilees[106] while all three are basically independent of each other and derived from the same earlier midrash.[107] Finally, J. T. Milik noted[108] that a T Naphtali fragment had been discovered at Qumran; it is unlike the Testaments' T Naphtali and the Naphtali traditions published by Gaster.[109] Milik's conclusion is similar to the one which he made concerning the Qumran T Levi fragment; the Testaments of the Twelve Patriarchs is not at Qumran and is, therefore, Christian or non-Palestinian.

In 1957 M. de Jonge gave a lecture[110] updating his findings of 1953 in the light of more recent scholarship, not the least of which was that of Milik. After a recapitulation of his earlier position,[111] de Jonge discusses the two major problems with his composition theory. First, D. R. Jones had argued that the existence of the Levi-Judah pattern in some instances with no Christian alterations points to an originally Jewish Testaments. Against this position de Jonge repeats what he had said already in 1953, i.e., the Levi-Judah pattern comes from one of the sources used by the Christian writer.[112] Second, Sparks had said there was too much material in the Testaments which was not necessarily Christian. Here de Jonge concedes that he has not paid enough attention to oral tradition and the possibility of its growth into a document whose last stage is the Christian Testaments.[113]

Next, de Jonge admits that he had not treated the Qumran materials with sufficient seriousness in his earlier study.[114] Now he affirms Milik's work[115] and approves of Otzen's care in showing parallels between Qumran and the Testaments without insisting that they have the same historical roots.[116] At this point he states two important principles of method: first, parallels do not signify dependencies; second, given the presence of clearly Christian materials in a document, it may not be said that materials less clearly Christian are not Christian.[117]

De Jonge concludes his discussion with a revision of his views concerning the date of writing of the Testaments. Because of the criticisms of Grant and Milik and the similarities between the Testaments and the Shepherd of Hermas, he now dates it before 190 C.E. The writer was not, however, a converted Qumran-Essene as Daniélou had suggested.[118]

It is not easy to tell where de Jonge had changed his position since 1953. He made an alteration in the date of composition of the Testaments, and he was concerned about those parts of the Levi-Judah pattern where no clear Christian reference was to be found. These latter were, he said, arguments in favor of a Jewish stage in the compilation of the document.[119] Similarly, Sparks had convinced de Jonge that the Christian Testaments might be a last stage of compilation.[120] Nevertheless, he concludes that

> these critical remarks do not, however, invalidate the conclusion that the Testaments of the Twelve Patriarchs, as we have them, are a Christian composition. Nor do they lend any support to the theory that a Jewish GRUNDSCHRIFT can be discovered after the removal of Christian interpolations, however extensive or however small.[121]

A. S. van der Woude, who also wrote in 1957,[122] could accept none of de Jonge's views.[123] In his first chapter he shows that the Qumran literature teaches a two-Messiah doctrine with the priestly Messiah having precedence.[124] In his second chapter he finds this doctrine in the Testaments and, using many of Charles' linguistic and text-critical results, analyzes various messianic passages. In each he shows that it is a priest rather than Jesus to whom the text referred originally. The Testaments comes, therefore, from Qumran.[125]

In 1958 M. Delcor[126] took up van der Woude's work. He affirms the two Messiahs at Qumran[127] and the Jewish nature of much of the apparently Christian material of the Testaments,[128] adding beyond van der Woude that the meal in T Levi 8:4-5 was not the Christian Eucharist but the Qumran table fellowship.[129] F. M. Cross used Milik's fragments to assert that they prove the origin of the Testaments at Qumran.[130] Cross gives no indication, however, why they prove this, nor does he deal with Milik's own contention to the contrary.[131]

In the same year a less simple evaluation of the relationship between Qumran and the Testaments appeared in Part IV of M-A. Chevallier's study.[132] Chevallier first shows that the Testaments and Qumran have much in common in terms of milieu,[133] theology,[134] and ethics.[135] He then indicates that even with these many parallels, there are also such strong differences that a close relationship between them is excluded. Among these differences he notes the following: first, demonology/angelology, cosmology, resurrection, and eschatology play a far greater part in the Testaments than at Qumran. Second, moral regimentation and ritual demands are important at Qumran but not in the Testaments. Third, the exegesis of the latter is haggadic, while that of the former is akin to pesher.[136] Chevallier admits, however, that such extensive differences might still be explainable in terms of development within the thinking of the Qumran community.[137] In his brief discussion of the two Messiahs in the Testaments and Qumran he concludes that in the Testaments the priestly Messiah takes precedence.[138] On this point he agrees with Kuhn and van der Woude. But Chevallier notes that in Qumran Aaron-Israel do not receive the separate treatment afforded them in the Testaments. Rather, it appears that the Messiah is still awaited and that Aaron and Israel designate respectively the whole priestly rule and the laity of the community.[139] Chevallier then asks whether the Teacher is the messianic figure at Qumran (Dupont-Sommer), but gives no direct answer.[140]

Without reaching a definite conclusion about the relationship between the Testaments and Qumran, Chevallier moves on to his central concern — the connection between the Spirit and Messiah in the Testaments[141] and at Qumran,[142] and the use made of Psalm 2 and Isaiah 11 in this connection. According to Chevallier, the two clearest messianic texts, T Levi 18:2-14 and T Judah 24,[143] are marked by three distinctive early Christian elements: first, they tell how the Spirit is given to the Messiah; second, they say the Spirit is given to men by the Messiah; and third, they speak of the adoption of believers.[144] Because the three elements are integral to the messianic texts, these are thoroughly Christian. This is not proof, however, that the whole of the Testaments was originally Christian.[145]

Chevallier's most distinctive conclusions come, however, in his discussion of the Spirit-Messiah at Qumran. Because CD 2:12 seems to indicate that the Messiah is the giver of the Spirit (as in the New Testament and T Judah 24:2b), Chevallier concludes that the Damascus Document may be a Christian writing.[146] Similarly, 1 QS 4:20-23 appears to be a gnostic reworking of Jesus' baptism.[147] What does this mean? Qumran may be a Jewish-Christian community![148]

Each of the first four chapters of this study concluded with a rather clearly defined period in the history of Testaments research. This is not true of the present one. As indicated at its beginning, the primary characteristic of the years from 1952 until 1958 was the rise of interest in the Testaments as related to Qumran and early Christianity. Negatively, it was marked partially by the back seat given to the Charles position and those who had held it for forty years. However, 1958 indicates no break in the general direction of the discussion; indeed, the first scholar to be dealt with in the following pages wrote also in 1958. Thus there is a definite continuity between this and the next phase of the discussion, which is characterized by increased intensity of the dispute between the advocates of Qumran and the advocates of Christian origins, as well as by a stronger interest in positions similar to those of R. H. Charles.

FOOTNOTES

[1]See p. 37 of this study.

[2]C. Rabin, "The 'Teacher of Righteousness' in the 'Testaments of the Twelve Patriarchs'?" *JJS* 3 (1952) 127-28. See also C. Rabin, *The Zadokite Documents* (Oxford: Clarendon, 1954) 83 for a list of parallels.

[3]Jean-Paul Audet, "Affinités littéraires et doctrinales du Manuel de discipline," *RB* 59 (1952) 219-38. On p. 238 he dates the original Two Ways in the early first century C. E. in Palestine-Syria.

[4]Audet, "Affinités," *RB* 60 (1953) 41-82.

[5]Ibid., 68, 80. There is some indication of this in the first part of the article (*RB* 59 233). K. G. Kuhn ("Jesus in Gethsemane," *EvT* 12 [1952] 260-85) at about the same time dealt with the question of the dualism of Qumran, the Testaments, and Shepherd of Hermas, in order to show that Mark 14:38 is an interpolation. Kuhn believes that the body-spirit dichotomy expressed in these texts is the product of Persian dualism, with Qumran the source of the Markan interpolation.

[6]André Dupont-Sommer, *Nouveaux aperçus sur des manuscrits de la mer Morte* (Paris: Maisonneuve, 1953) 63-84.

[7]Ibid., 63.

[8]Ibid., 64.

[9]Ibid., 68-73.

[10]Ibid., 75-76.

[11]Ibid., 78-83.

[12]Ibid., 83.

[13]Benedikt Otzen, "Die neugefundenen hebraïschen Sektenschriften und die Testamente der zwölf Patriarchen," *ST* 7 (1953) 125-57.

[14]Ibid., 155. "It may not be asserted that the Testaments of the Twelve Patriarchs and the new [Qumran] texts either come from the same sect, or have the same historical background or mirror the same historical events."

[15]Ibid., 126-34.

[16]Ibid., 135-42.

[17]Ibid., 142-44.

[18]Ibid., 145-51.

[19]Ibid., 147.

[20]Ibid., 147-49.

[21]Ibid., 149-50.

[22]Ibid., 150-51.

[23]Ibid., 153-54.

[24]Ibid., 154-55.

[25]M. de Jonge, *The Testaments of the Twelve Patriarchs: A Study of Their Text, Composition and Origin* (Assen: van Gorcum, 1953).

[26]He has said on various occasions since 1953 that he paid too little attention to them.

[27]M. de Jonge, *The Testaments of the Twelve Patriarchs* 11-12.

[28]Ibid., 13-22.

[29]Ibid., 22.

[30]Ibid., 23-31.

[31]Ibid., 31-34.

[32]Ibid., 34.

[33]Ibid., 35-36.

[34]Ibid., 36.

[35]It may be helpful to recall that F. Schnapp had based his Jewish origin theory solely on literary-critical evidence. It is only with Conybeare, Preuschen, Bousset, and Charles that text criticism became an issue.

[36]See pp. 24, 26 of this study.

[37]De Jonge, *The Testaments of the Twelve Patriarchs* 39-42.

[38]Ibid., 40-42.

[39]Ibid., 42.

[40]See pp. 22, 24 of this study.

[41]De Jonge, *The Testaments of the Twelve Patriarchs* 52.

[42]Ibid., 53.

[43]Ibid., 55-57.

[44]Ibid., 57.

[45]Ibid., 62.

[46]Ibid., 64.

[47]Ibid., 66.

[48]Ibid., 71.

[49]Ibid., 73.

[50]Ibid., 77.

[51]Ibid., 81.

[52]Ibid., 85.

[53]Ibid., 87.

[54]Ibid., 88.

[55]Ibid., 90.

[56]Ibid., 96, 98.

[57]Ibid., 101-06.

[58]Ibid., 110.

[59]Ibid., 121-25. These parallels are as follows: T Dan 5:6 and Irenaeus associate Dan and Satan; T Benj 11:1, Tertullian, and Hippolytus use Gen 49:27 in reference to Paul; the Joseph-Christ typology appears first in Hippolytus and Cyprian; and Levi-Judah in relationship to the Messiah appears first in Hippolytus.

[60]This is similar to Sinker's view of the Christian author of the Testaments. See p. 14 of the present study.

[61]De Jonge, *The Testaments of the Twelve Patriarchs* 125-28.

[62]J. W. Doeve, rev. of M. de Jonge, *The Testaments of the Twelve Patriarchs, Nederlands theologisch Tijdschrift* 9 (1954-1955) 49-52.

[63]D. R. Jones, rev. of M. de Jonge, *The Testaments of the Twelve Patriarchs, Theology* 57 (1954) 390-92.

[64]Karl Georg Kuhn, "Die beiden Messias Aarons und Israels," *NTS* 1 (1955) 168-79. An English translation appears in Krister Stendahl, ed., *The Scrolls and the New Testament* (New York: Harper and Brothers, 1957) 54-64.

[65]Kuhn, "Die beiden Messias," 168-71.

[66]Ibid., 172.

[67]Ibid., 173. "Their language and thought world show in detail that the Testaments of the Twelve Patriarchs belong within the circle of the Essene texts."

[68]P. Hartmut Aschermann, "Die paränetischen Formen der 'Testamente der zwölf Patriarchen' und ihr Nachwirken in der frühchristlichen Mahnung." Th.D. dissertation, Humboldt Universität-Berlin, 1955. I want to record my appreciation to Professor de Jonge for allowing me to borrow a copy of this dissertation sent to him by Dr. Aschermann.

[69]Ibid., 2-3.

[70]Ibid., 5-27.

[71]Ibid., 8.

[72]Ibid., 7.

[73]Ibid., 11-25.

[74]Ibid., 21-23.

[75]Ibid., 25-26.

[76]Ibid., 29-99.

[77]Ibid., 30-44.

[78]Ibid., 44-48.

[79]Ibid., 49-55.

[80]Ibid., 63-75.

[81]Ibid., 73-74.

[82]Ibid., 77-98.

[83]Ibid., 98-99.

[84]Ibid., 100-55.

[85]Ibid., 100.

[86]Ibid., 125.

[87]Ibid., 101.

[88]Ibid., 131.

[89]Ibid., 101.

[90]Ibid., 110.

[91]Robert M. Grant, rev. of M. de Jonge, *The Testaments, VC* 9 (1955) 185-86.

[92]Jean Daniélou, rev. of M. de Jonge, *The Testaments, RSR* 43 (1955) 564-67.

[93]Ibid., 565. In his later *Les manuscrits de la mer Morte et les origines du christianisme* (Paris: Editions de l'Orante, 1957) 109-11, Daniélou adds that the writer was a Christian converted from Qumran, since he uses its teachings.

[94]J. T. Milik, "Le Testament de Lévi en araméen; fragment de la grotte 4 de Qumrân," *RB* 62 (1955) 398-406.

[95]Ibid., 399.

[96]Ibid., 405-06. "Let us keep in mind finally that in the Qumran '*lots*' there are no remains of an original semitic Testaments of the Twelve Patriarchs. Given the extreme wealth and variety of the work, this practically excludes a pre-Christian and Palestinian origin for the writing. And everything leads one to believe that the Testaments are a Jewish-Christian composition using Jewish writings."

[97]J. T. Milik, rev. of M. de Jonge, *The Testaments*, *RB* 62 (1955) 297-98.

[98]Ibid., 298.

[99]Ibid.

[100]H. F. D. Sparks, rev. of M. de Jonge, *The Testaments*, *JTS*, n.s. 6 (1955) 289.

[101]Ibid., 289-90.

[102]Pierre Grelot, "Le testament araméen de Lévi est-il traduit de l'hébreu?" *Revue des études juives* 14 (1955) 91-99.

[103]According to Grelot the Testaments has only a résumé of this passage (T Levi 11:4).

[104]Ibid., 97.

[105]Pierre Grelot, "Notes sur le testament araméen de Lévi: fragment de la Bodleian Library, Colonne a," *RB* 63 (1956) 391-406.

[106]Ibid., 402-03.

[107]Ibid., 404.

[108]J. T. Milik, "'Prière de Nabonide' et autres écrits d'un cycle de Daniel: fragments de Qumrân 4," *RB* 63 (1956) 407, n. 1.

[109]See p. 22 of this study.

[110]M. de Jonge, "The Testaments of the Twelve Patriarchs and the New Testament," TU 73 (1959) 546-56.

[111]Ibid., 547-49.

[112]Ibid., 549-50.

[113]Ibid., 550-51.

[114]Ibid., 551.

[115]Ibid., 551-52.

[116]Ibid., 552-54.

[117]Ibid., 554.

[118]Ibid., 555.

[119]Ibid., 550.

[120]Ibid.

[121]Ibid.

[122]A. S. van der Woude, *Die messianischen Vorstellungen der Gemeinde von Qumrân* (Assen: van Gorcum, 1957) 190-216.

[123]This is with the exception (pp. 191-94) that both agree a Jewish original cannot be recovered. According to van der Woude (p. 193) the original Jewish Testaments was probably reworked before the addition of Christian interpolations.

[124]Van der Woude, 190. Writing in the same year as van der Woude, Raymond E. Brown ("The Messianism of Qumrân," *CBQ* 19 [1957] 53-82) also defended the existence of a two-Messiah doctrine at Qumran. After indicating the causes for the rise of the priestly Messiah in the period subsequent to 585 B.C.E., Brown showed this nascent figure in the later OT writings. Concerning the Testaments he simply stated that the two-Messiah doctrine is to be found there among the writings of the Pseudepigrapha. Again in the same year Kurt Schubert ("Testamentum Juda 24 im Lichte der Texte von Chirbet Qumran," *Wiener Zeitschrift für die Kunde des Morgenlands* 53 [1957] 227-236), assuming the Qumran origin of the Testaments, argued that a doctrine of two Messiahs could be found in T Judah 24 if this text were retranslated into the original Hebrew of the Qumran Community.

[125]Ibid., 215.

[126]M. Delcor, "Dix ans de travaux sur les manuscrits de Qumrân," *Revue thomiste* 58 (1958) 734-79.

[127] Ibid., 771.

[128] Ibid., 775.

[129] Ibid.

[130] F. M. Cross, *The Ancient Library of Qumran and Modern Biblical Studies* (London: Gerald Duckworth, 1958) 149, n. 6.

[131] Millar Burrows (*More Light on the Dead Sea Scrolls* [New York: Viking, 1958] 179) concluded that Milik was correct in seeing the Testaments as Jewish-Christian.

[132] Max-Alain Chevallier, *L'esprit et le messie dans le bas judaïsme et le Nouveau Testament* (Paris: Presses universitaires de France, 1958).

[133] Ibid., 117-18.

[134] Ibid.

[135] Ibid., 119.

[136] Ibid., 119-20.

[137] Ibid., 120.

[138] Ibid., 121.

[139] Ibid., 121-22.

[140] Ibid., 123-24.

[141] Ibid., 125-33.

[142] Ibid., 134-43.

[143] Ibid., 126.

[144] Ibid., 129-30.

[145] Ibid., 132.

[146] Ibid., 136-39.

[147] Ibid., 142.

[148] Ibid., 142-43.

CHAPTER VI

1958 to the Present: Qumran or Christian Origins Continued, and Charles Reintroduced

It was indicated at the end of the last chapter that the studies to be reviewed in the following pages would be marked by both an increased intensity of debate between scholars supporting Qumran and Christian origins for the Testaments, and by a renewed interest in positions similar to those of R. H. Charles which believe the Testaments to have originated in non-sectarian Judaism. Moreover, these studies are marked by the developing complexity of research as it interweaves the three origins theories proposed by scholarship. These developments appear in the brief span between 1958 and 1960.

M. Philonenko, J. Liver, M. de Jonge, and F.-M. Braun: The Authorship Logjam

M. Philonenko's main purpose was to show, on a larger scale than Dupont-Sommer, that the messianic interpolations in the Testaments do not refer to Jesus but to the Qumran Teacher.[1] He begins his discussion of the relationship between the Qumran literature and the Testaments with three assumptions: first, Qumran and the Testaments have some form of common origin, particularly since the Qumran finds yielded a T Levi and a T Naphtali;[2] second, Charles correctly held that the Testaments had been written originally in Hebrew; and third, the Testaments contains Jewish interpolations.[3] Philonenko lists these interpolations, noting that a common characteristic is the Sin-Exile-Return pattern defined by de Jonge. On the basis of the similarity between this pattern and sections of the Psalms of Solomon, he argues that the exile theme is a vaticinium ex eventu concerning the capture of Jerusalem by Pompey in 63 B.C.E. He concludes, therefore, that the Jewish interpolations form a redaction of the Testaments after 63 B.C.E.; the reference to Herod the Great in T Judah 22:2 implies a time of writing not long after 37 B.C.E.[4]

Philonenko mentions three other themes introduced by the Jewish interpolator-redactor, i.e., the Levi-Judah pattern, the resurrection motif, and the universalism motif. Because the so-called Christian interpolations appear only within these Jewish interpolations, Philonenko argues that they are not Christian at all but belong rather to the Jewish interpolation-redaction stage.[5] Here Philonenko comes to his central concern — showing that the christological interpolations do not refer to Jesus but to the Teacher of Qumran. In order to do this, Philonenko devotes the rest of his study to analyzing various texts heretofore regarded by most scholars as Christian.[6] He concludes that there are no significant Christian interpolations in the Testaments and that the Teacher "christology" of this writing is helpful in establishing a history and theology of the Qumran Community.[7]

Philonenko's study is a modification of the theory first presented by Schnapp — that the Christian interpolations in the Testaments are found in the Jewish, apocalyptically-oriented interpolations. Philonenko's modification of Schnapp is two-fold: first, these Jewish interpolations are a product of Qumran; second, the so-called Christian interpolations within these belong to the Qumran interpolations. Thus, there are two stages in the development of the present Testaments, the second of which is Qumran-Jewish. The first stage is evidently of little interest to Philonenko, since he nowhere gives it a clear place in Jewish history.

It was specifically this first stage or original Testaments, however, which interested J. Liver in his discussion of "The Doctrine of the Two Messiahs in Sectarian Literature in the Time of the Second Commonwealth."[8] Published at about the same time as Philonenko's articles, it provides a rather perfect complement to his study, because it argues on the basis of the Levi-Judah passages that this document is a product of the Qumran Community.

Liver first discusses the messianism of the Qumran literature, arguing on the basis of the 1Q texts that this community awaited a more prominent priestly and less prominent kingly Messiah.[9] Finding, however, that the 4Q texts stress Davidic future rule in their interpretation of various OT passages, Liver concludes that between 1Q and 4Q there exists a development in the messianism of the Qumran Community.[10]

Given this analysis, Liver devotes the remainder of his study to the Testaments. He first states that, granted the presence of the two-Messiah doctrine at Qumran, there is no reason to believe either the Judah Messiah (Charles) or the Levi Messiah (Kohler, Ginzberg) is a later interpolation.[11] Second, in a study of Levi-Judah passages[12] he finds a consistent picture of the Testaments' messianism; Levi is the priestly Messiah superior to and separate from the royal Messiah.[13]

Finally, on the basis of his study Liver draws various important conclusions: first, the priest became the major figure in Israel after the Exile;[14] second, the founders of the Qumran Community were Zadokites opposed to the new Hasmonean priesthood;[15] third, these founders stressed the priestly Messiah but, because of tradition, maintained also a royal Messiah;[16] fourth, differences between 1Q and 4Q indicate a return to the more traditional messianism, probably as the Hasmoneans declined;[17] fifth, Qumran and the

Testaments have an identical two-Messiah doctrine;[18] and sixth, only within the Qumran Community does such a doctrine appear.[19] Thus, whereas Philonenko had assigned only certain interpolations in the Testaments to the Qumran Community, Liver ascribed the whole document to that group.

In 1960 M. de Jonge once again took up the defense of his position, this time against the two major attacks which had been launched against him by van der Woude and Philonenko.[20] De Jonge first concerns himself with the four reasons why van der Woude had rejected his theory of an original Christian Testaments: (1) The Hebraisms of the document prove original Jewish authorship. Against this de Jonge says that the Testaments is Semitic and not translation Greek, and that it uses Hebrew sources in various places.[21] (2) The Armenian Version witnesses a less Christian document. Against this de Jonge simply notes that no case has been made for it.[22] (3) Many so-called Christian passages probably were not Christian. Here de Jonge repeats his very important point that it is not proper method to eliminate what is obviously Christian and then call Jewish that which is not obviously Christian nor Jewish. Rather, says de Jonge, given the existence of Christian materials, the burden of proof must fall upon the person who says that the remainder is not Christian.[23] (4) Since parts of the Levi-Judah pattern have no obvious Christian reference, there must have been an original Jewish Testaments. To this de Jonge responds, as he had in 1957, that such a pattern is evidence for a pre-Christian Testaments; nonetheless, such a pre-Christian stage would be quite unrecoverable given the freedom of the Christian writer with his sources.[24]

De Jonge next makes four major criticisms of Philonenko's method. First, he repeats his contention that similar ideas in separate sources do not prove the dependence of one source upon the other.[25] Second, he says Philonenko erred in taking Testaments passages out of their context.[26] Third, he erred again in thinking that the supposed Christian materials exist only in the passages with which he had worked.[27] Fourth, Philonenko was guilty of circular argumentation when, after admitting that Qumran and the Testaments do not have the same christology, he said that the Testaments represented later christological development within the Qumran Community.[28]

Finally, as indicated above, de Jonge considers passages from the document itself in support of his view. For example, in his discussion of Philonenko's position that the Joseph material refers to the Teacher,[29] de Jonge concludes that "the contention that already in Qumran Joseph was regarded as a type of the Teacher of Righteousness seems to me to find as yet too little support in the available evidence."[30] Similarly, in his discussion of the Levi-Judah pattern in T Judah 24,[31] de Jonge concludes that it is a Christian passage into which "possibly material from the Qumran sect (or a related group) has been incorporated."[32] He then reaches the following conclusions about the Levi-Judah pattern and its significance for the question of the origins of the Testaments: first, Original Levi stressed the tribe of Levi and mentioned Judah only in passing; second, the Levi-Judah pattern was added later, probably from Original Naphtali, when the other testaments were added to Original Naphtali; third, the Levi-Judah pattern in the original Testaments placed Levi above Judah; fourth, Levi and Judah originally represented tribes and not Messiahs; fifth, the present Testaments has a Christian-redacted Levi-Judah pattern; and sixth, the history of composition of the Testaments is complex and not fully traceable.[33]

In 1957 de Jonge had already made certain concessions about the possibility of the existence of a pre-Christian Testaments. In the article just discussed, therefore, he is not in opposition to van der Woude in terms of the possibility of such a pre-Christian document. He does, however, believe its recovery an impossibility. Nevertheless, de Jonge is firmly opposed to the views of Philonenko, because he has not shown that the Qumran Teacher is the Messiah of the Testaments.

The year 1960 had not yet ended when F.-M. Braun's study on the Testaments was published.[34] While Braun accepts certain elements from the arguments of de Jonge, van der Woude, Dupont-Sommer, and Philonenko, he does this only to use them to reject the origin theories proposed by each of these scholars; he has a new theory. Braun begins his discussion with a total rejection of the possibility that the Testaments is a Christian document. In a comparison with the Didache, Barnabas, and Hermas, Braun concludes that the Christian material in the Testaments is superficial as compared to the Didache, etc.,[35] and that its paraenesis stresses obedience to the Law unlike the Didache, etc.[36]

Next, Braun examines the relationship between the Testaments and Qumran literature, finding close parallels between these in their moral teaching.[37] The one exception is the teaching on neighbor-love and the stranger; here he says that the New Testament and Testaments are similar and unlike Qumran. He does cite rabbinic texts to show, however, that the Judaism of the period (if not Qumran) was interested also in neighbor-love and the stranger.[38]

But Qumran and the Testaments have still more in common than moral teachings. An analysis of T Judah 24:1-6[39] and T Levi 18[40] reveals that in these passages as well as at Qumran the doctrine of two Messiahs is present.[41] Does this then mean that the Testaments is a product of Qumran? No; if de Jonge was wrong, so was Dupont-Sommer, because Qumran and the Testaments have three major differences between them. First, the Testaments is not rigorous in its stress on Torah study;[42] second, it has no sense of escape from the world;[43] third, it is open to the Gentiles.[44] It is this third point which serves as Braun's clue to the origin of the Testaments. Universalism is primarily a tendency of Hellenistic Judaism.[45] Therefore, the writer of the Testaments was a diaspora Jew of priestly or Palestinian origin, who wrote with knowledge of haggadah, apocalyptic, and the Qumran teachings.[46]

De Jonge had suggested that the writer of the Testaments used Hellenistic Jewish traditions and already in 1810 C. I. Nitzsch had proposed Alexandria as the place of writing of the Testaments; but Braun's theory of origin, taking in as it does elements of previous theories, is quite clearly new.

The next year (1961) was concerned solely, however, with the work of Philonenko. Regardless of de Jonge's and Braun's criticisms, P. Geoltrain[47] accepted each of the arguments of Philonenko that the Teacher is more clearly the messianic referent in the Testaments than is Jesus; but others were not of the same opinion. M. E. Boismard criticized Philonenko on two grounds: first, many of his Teacher texts are Christian; second, various statements made concerning the Messiah in the Testaments are nowhere said about the Teacher in the Qumran texts.[48] P. Wernberg-Møller offered a similar criticism, noting also that Philonenko used questionable translations of his texts to show the Teacher's presence in the Testaments.[49] Then in 1962 G. Bernini[50] questioned Philonenko on the grounds that the christologies of the Testaments and Qumran are very different. G. Delling noted that even if the Testaments were written in Hebrew it might still be a Christian document.[51] L. Rost, impressed with the Levi fragments from Qumran, concluded that the Testaments must have been written by a group geographically near to the Qumran Community;[52] however, because the Testaments itself had not been found at Qumran, he said that Philonenko was hasty in placing it there.[53] Similarly, M. Smith saw parallels between the Testaments and Qumran, but would not say that Qumran was its place of origin. Smith also accepted some of Charles' and Bickerman's historical allusions in the Testaments as referring to the Hasmonean period; nonetheless, because of the framework of the present text, he concluded that the document in its present form is Christian.[54]

It should be apparent that between 1961 and 1962 M. Philonenko's study was not well received. Already in 1960, with the studies of de Jonge and Braun, this negative reception had begun. In the same year Braun had flatly rejected de Jonge's position, and in 1962 we have de Jonge's response to Braun.[55] He agrees with Braun that the Testaments did not originate at Qumran[56] and that it may well be a product of the Hellenistic milieu.[57] Against Braun, however, he says once more that it is improper to remove the clearly Christian materials and then call the rest Jewish.[58] Moreover, no Jew ever existed who fits the description of the author proposed by Braun.[59]

Thus, by 1962 there was a definite logjam in the question of the origin of the Testaments. De Jonge continued to defend the thesis that the Testaments was a Christian compilation, and Braun admitted the existence of extensive Christian additions in the Testaments while arguing that the original document was produced in the Jewish Diaspora. Philonenko was vague concerning the original Testaments but quite sure that the present document represented the work of the Qumran Community; and Liver insisted that the original document itself arose within or very near that community. We see therefore that de Jonge, Braun, Philonenko, and Liver each proposed different and generally irreconcilable theories about the origin of the Testaments.

It should not be surprising, then, that the logjam of 1962 had definite effects upon the study of the Testaments during the remainder of the decade. The immediate effect was that scholarship moved away from attempts to resolve directly the question of the origin of the Testaments. In place of these, various analyses of themes and forms within the Testaments appeared; and soon a new text-critical interest developed. Thus, the logjam also provided an impetus for motif-, form-, and text-critical work which would be valuable in the long run for the origins question.

The Analysis of Individual Motifs and
Forms in the Testaments

B. Vawter was one of the first scholars in recent years to discuss the Testaments strictly from the perspective of a theological motif.[60] According to him the theme of levitical messianism appears nowhere in Jewish literature including Qumran.[61] It makes its first appearance within Christianity, particularly in Hippolytus (who bases it upon Luke 1:5, 36)[62] and in the Testaments' Christian sections, T Judah 24:1-3 and T Levi 18:6-12.[63]

In the same year R. Le Déaut examined the figure of Melchizedek,[64] indicating at the outset that in Ambrose and the Apostolic Constitutions this figure is given the title *Summus Sacerdos*.[65] He then seeks the origin of the Melchizedek-*Summus Sacerdos* theme in Judaism, arguing that its use by the author of Hebrews shows its use also by his Jewish opponents.[66] Le Déaut finally notes the presence of the theme in the earliest Roman canon with close parallels in T Levi 3:5-6.[67] Like Vawter, Le Déaut offered no conclusions about the origins of the Testaments; both studies are important, however, in showing that certain theological themes in the Testaments have their best counterparts not in Jewish but in Christian literature.[68]

Similarly, in 1962 J. Gnilka published a study of the Benedictus (Luke 1:67-79)[69] in which he gives careful consideration to the messianic conception of the ἀνατολὴ ἐξ ὕψους. Gnilka finds the use of the conception in Luke to be like that in T Judah 24:1.[70] Moreover, the Testaments as a whole has four themes in common with the Benedictus: first, the Messiah as a rising star; second, διὰ σπλάγχνα ἐλέος; third, ἐπισκέπτεσθαι; fourth Κύριος as a title for God and the Messiah.[71] Consequently Gnilka concludes that the present Testaments is Christian (vs. Philonenko),[72] Jewish-Christian by content,[73] and closely related to the Benedictus community.[74]

In 1963 three articles appeared which dealt in a minor way with the Testaments through themes related to it. Gnilka wrote concerning 2 Cor 6:14 — 7:1, arguing that these verses are an interpolation.[75] Because of their concern for the separation of the holy[76] and their Qumran-Testaments form of dualism,[77] he concludes that these verses were added to Second Corinthians by a Christian influenced by Qumran and the Testaments.[78] Again, M. Rese argued that T Benj 3:8 has no reference to a Messiah from Joseph,[79] and G. Widengren repeated Charles' view that the Testaments contains a levitical royal messianism.[80]

In 1964 the second edition of K. Baltzer's study of the covenant formula (*Bundesformular*) was published.[81] Though without citing evidence, Baltzer asserts that the Testaments is a Jewish writing with Christian interpolations.[82] As such it illustrates very well the four-part covenant formula of the OT with its 1) narration of the pre-history, 2) description of the relationship of the covenant partners, 3) regulations of the covenant, and 4) blessings/curses for obedience/disobedience toward these regulations.[83] The main value of Baltzer's work as it relates to the Testaments is that it defends the integrity of the whole document by showing that the apocalyptic sections (vs. Schnapp and Philonenko) are essential to its overall structure.[84] Thus Baltzer makes sense of the whole and gives it a uniform purpose.

Also in 1964[85] the first indication of a renewed interest in the text criticism of the Testaments appeared with the publication of M. de Jonge's edition of his preferred text of the Testaments, Cambridge University Library MS Ff I.24.[86] C. Burchard responded soon with a positive review, commenting also upon Charles' poor choice of Greek texts and his own preference for the Greek Group B MSS of which MS Ff I.24 is a prime witness.[87] At about the same time Burchard published descriptions of a 17th century MS of the Testaments belonging to Group B and of a more modern MS related to Group A.[88]

Then in a third article[89] he entered into the 1966 debate between K. Koch and J. Jeremias concerning the existence of a pre-Christian lamb-redeemer figure in T Jos 19:8. Where Koch[90] had argued for such a pre-Christian figure on the basis of Charles' version of this verse, Jeremias insisted from MS Ff I.24[91] and the word "virgin" that the text is Christian.[92] Burchard agrees with Jeremias.[93]

In the same year, A. J. B. Higgins[94] returns to the theme of the priestly Messiah, finding with Vawter that such a figure does not exist at Qumran.[95] He then analyzes those texts in the Testaments claimed as evidence for the existence of a priestly Messiah. He says that T Reuben 6:7-12 is a Christian text with no levitical Messiah,[96] and that T Levi 18:1-3,6-9 and T Judah 24:1-3 refer to Jesus.[97] He concludes: first, the Testaments is a Christian document with pre-Christian elements in it; second, T Reuben 6:7-12, T Levi 18, and T Judah 24 praise the figure of Levi, but not as Messiah; third, the Levi-Judah pattern places Levi above Judah, but again not as Messiah. According to Higgins, therefore, the Testaments and Qumran are similar in having no levitical Messiah; differences between them, however, preclude any close relationship.[98]

Finally, in 1967 R. A. Stewart[99] published the last of the motif studies of the 1960s related to the Testaments. Stewart's theme is the sinless high priest; and his purpose is to find the Jewish source from which Hebrews borrowed it. An analysis of the OT,[100] Ben Sirach,[101] Qumran,[102] Josephus,[103] Philo,[104] and the rabbis[105] leads Stewart to conclude that among these sources Philo alone, and here only in an abstract form, has such a doctrine. Not satisfied with any of these sources, Stewart then examines T Levi 18 on the assumption that the Testaments and this passage are Jewish.[106] Finding the sinless high priest in T Levi 18, Stewart concludes therefore that this passage (possibly also Philo) is the Jewish source for the Christian usage of the sinless high priest motif in the Epistle to the Hebrews.[107]

Thus, like the motif studies of Vawter, Le Déaut, Gnilka, Jeremias, and Burchard, Stewart's analysis provides another case in which a particular Testaments theme seems to have its clearest counterpart not in Jewish but in Christian literature. On the other hand, the form-critical studies of Baltzer and Steck (see note 82) trace Testaments forms to their OT and Jewish sources without, however, denying a place to these same forms in early Christianity.

Significant Text-Critical Developments

As indicated previously, a renewed interest in the textual criticism of the Testaments appeared in 1964 with the publication of the Cambridge text and Burchard's brief discussions. Then, between 1967 and 1972 five very significant studies dealt at length with the text-critical issue. C. Burchard and M. Stone worked with the Armenian Version, A Hultgård with the Greek and Armenian, E. Turdeanu with the Slavonic, and H. J. de Jonge with the Greek.

In his introduction, Burchard[108] makes four important assertions: first, Burkitt, Hunkin, and de Jonge have shown conclusively that among the Greek MSS Group B is superior to Charles' Group A; second, Charles' Hebrew recension theory is wrong, because Greek A and Greek B do not have the characteristics of two Hebrew recensions and the Greek Testaments does not appear to be a translation; third, Charles errs in following Conybeare's theory that the lacunae of the Armenian Version witness to a less Christian Testaments, because these lacunae do not correspond particularly to the supposed Christian interpolations; and fourth, Charles has not dealt sufficiently with the Slavonic Version.[109] On this basis Burchard concludes that a new edition of the Testaments is needed in which the Greek Group B MSS provide the basic text and the Armenian and Slavonic readings the apparatus.[110]

Burchard lists the forty-five known MSS of the Armenian Version[111] and tries to date the translation of the Testaments into Armenian.[112] While Burchard says there is no proof that this translation took place between 500 and 700 C.E.,[113] he believes that the Testaments was translated by 1100 and probably much earlier. The Armenian Version thus pre-dates the earliest Greek text (MS Ff I.24 — 10th century), and for this reason is valuable in the textual criticism of the Testaments.

Burchard then considers the textual history of this version.[114] He begins with a recapitulation of R. H. Charles' position that the Armenian MSS may be separated into six families and that these families may be separated into recensions A^α and A^β, of which A^β is a longer text, always appears in Biblical MSS, and is generally superior to A^α.[115] Having described Charles' position, Burchard begins his own examination of the Armenian MSS, using a far larger store of MSS than Charles had. His method is as follows: first, he observes that the Testaments sometimes appears in the MSS with Joseph and Aseneth (JA), sometimes with Joseph and Aseneth and the Life of Joseph (LJos), and sometimes in Biblical MSS with or without Joseph and Aseneth.[116] Second, he observes that in twenty-two MSS where the Testaments and Joseph and Aseneth appear together one of three sequences is present; Testaments-JA, LJos-JA-Testaments, or Testaments-LJos-JA.[117] Third, because all three of these appear in early MSS, Burchard concludes that the Testaments and JA have the same textual history and that, therefore, we may use the better researched JA textual history to study that of the Testaments.[118]

Burchard now evaluates Charles' six families of Armenian MSS. His first family (A^a)[119] does not appear with Joseph and Aseneth, unlike all of Charles' other MSS). Burchard's conclusion: A^a is a separate family just as his predecessor said.[120] Charles' second family (A^{hk}) offers the pattern of LJos-JA-Testaments. It too is, as Charles said, a separate family.[121] His third family (A^b) is unique because it includes no Bible MSS, and has the order JA-Testaments; it is therefore a separate family.[122] Burchard makes similar observations concerning A^{cd}, A^{efg}, and A^{b*}, and concludes that Charles' six families of MSS do exist.[123] He then notes, however, that the Armenian MSS Erewan 1500 and 353 fit none of Charles' families and may be a seventh family.[124]

Granted that Charles designated the families correctly, Burchard next evaluates the description of the two recensions which Charles had found within the six families, i.e., recension A^α composed of MSS A^a, A^{hk}, and A^b, and recension A^β composed of MSS A^{cd}, A^{efg}, and A^{b*}.[125] In order to understand Burchard's method it is important to keep in mind his presupposed work on the textual families within Joseph and Aseneth. These are designated by Burchard as JA a-e, each letter representing one of five Joseph and Aseneth text families.[126]

First, Charles had said A^{hk} and A^b are similar; and Burchard agrees because neither appears in a Biblical MS, while both have the LJos-JA-Testaments order and begin the Testaments with T Simeon.[127] Second, A^{efg} and A^{b*} are closely related because they have the Testaments-JA order and correspond to the similar JA a and e.[128] Third, A^{efg} and A^{cd} are not as close as Charles indicated because the corresponding JA b and e are quite different; rather, A^{cd} and A^{ahkb} (LJos-JA-Testaments) are similar since A^{efg} has no LJos and is composed of later MSS.[129] Finally, Erewan 1500 is similar to A^{ahkb} and A^{cd}, having less in common with A^{efg} and A^{b*}. The former group (Erewan 1500, A^{ahkb}, A^{cd}) provides a very ancient textual witness.[130]

What does this mean for the two-recension theory proposed by Charles? Because the six families of MSS cross the supposed recensional lines between A^α and A^β, A^α and A^β themselves are nonexistent, as are the two recensions proposed by Charles on the basis of them.[131] The proper means, therefore, of reconstructing the Armenian Version is to develop an eclectic text using all of the MSS, keeping in mind that A^b and A^{b*} tend to be the poorest witnesses to the version and A^{cd} and Erewan 1500 the best. Burchard then gives examples of how Erewan 1500 improves Charles' texts of T Reuben and T Benjamin.[132]

Finally, rejecting Charles' text-critical analysis of the Armenian Version,[133] Burchard concludes that the eclectically derived Armenian Version should produce a text similar to the Greek MSS bdgkl (Group B and de Jonge's preferred sub-group δ) in a good state such as it might have had in the sixth or seventh century when translated into Armenian: "That is, the Armenian Version does not for the most part produce a better text than may be derived from the Greek witnesses but makes that text older and more certain."[134]

The same volume which contained Burchard's 1967 article also offered two others when published in 1969. Before discussing these, however, we shall examine the four remaining text-critical studies.

The purpose of M. Stone's work is made clear already in its long title, *The Testament of Levi: A First Study of the Armenian MSS of the Testaments of the XII Patriarchs in the Convent of St. James, Jerusalem, with Text, Critical Apparatus, Notes and Translation* (1969). In his first chapter Stone discusses each of the nineteen MSS of the Armenian Version known to him, unaware of the additional MSS used by Burchard. In introducing the MSS he indicates that the major value of this version is its greater age than the earliest known Greek MS. Stone says that de Jonge had "succeeded in showing, beyond any reasonable doubt, that the omission of Christian interpolations found in the Greek, insofar as such occurs in the Armenian, is for the most part secondary."[135] The Armenian Version does not witness, therefore, to an earlier, less Christian text.

He then discusses the characteristics of all of the MSS with their interrelationships. First studied is MS m which Stone found in Jerusalem. This is in many ways superior to all other Armenian MSS so far known and agrees with the Greek in various readings against all other Armenian witnesses.[136] Stone then collates MS m with each of the other Jerusalem MSS against the rest of these MSS and finds no particularly close relationship between MS m and any other Jerusalem MS.[137]

He next discusses the relationship between the recension A^α and A^β established by Preuschen and affirmed by Charles and de Jonge, saying with de Jonge that A^β is consistently superior.[138] According to Stone, therefore, two groups of Armenian MSS do exist; moreover, these have a common Armenian archetype. Listing five features of all Armenian MSS to show that this is the case, Stone draws the following conclusion:

> It appears from the comparison of NOPQR [Stone's Jerusalem Armenian MSS] with Charles' and Yovsep'ianc's collations of B*CDEFG, that these fall into the same group [A^β] as opposed to ABH(?K)S [A^α]. The latter are distinguished by omissions, changes of word order, periphrases, etc., all of which go beyond the normal processes of textual

evolution. It is therefore clear that this text form [A^α] is the result of deliberate
recensional activity. . . .[139]

Stone then discusses MS m, indicating that it is closest to the A^β MSS;[140]
however, MS m is free of five of the seven omissions in A^β of materials present
in A^α and the Greek MSS. In this instance A^α, supported by MS m, is to be
preferred; but MS m is not the *Vorlage* of A^α because of two instances in which
A^α and the Greek retain material omitted by MS m and A^β.[141] Stone argues,
therefore,

> that M, which shows a text basically like the better text-type known to Charles, i.e., β,
> but containing a large number of readings superior to all the MSS of β, is a text better
> than any published. The corroboration of some of its readings in the other text-type,
> which in spite of its general inferiority, preserves at certain points readings better than .
> those of β, is of interest. It shows that the unique superior readings of M can be regarded
> as reflecting an Old Armenian tradition and are not the result of later reworking. This
> same coincidence also shows that those readings of α which appear to reflect the Greek,
> and which are found neither in M, nor in N-G must also be taken seriously.[142]

He then introduces the Armenian text of T Levi which fills the remainder of
the study. For the text and translation of Armenian A^β of T Levi he uses MS m
with the other A^β MSS in the apparatus;[143] for A^α he uses Jerusalem MS 939.[144]

It is apparent that Burchard and Stone, working separately and with
different MSS, came to similar conclusions on many issues raised by the
Armenian Version. They agreed that the major value of this version is that it is
a translation of a Greek MS of the Testaments more ancient by centuries than
the earliest extant Greek MS. Again, they agreed that de Jonge's position
concerning the relationship and value of the Greek text and versions is correct.
That is, Burchard saw the Armenian omissions as secondary and Stone
considered MS m, similar to the best Greek MSS, as the best Armenian witness.
They disagreed, however, concerning the existence of true recensions in the
Armenian Version. Burchard denied their existence, saying that the
preference in readings should not be given on the basis of a theoretically
preferable recension but on the basis of individual readings collated with the
Greek Group B. Stone on the other hand, like Charles and de Jonge, affirmed
the existence of A^α and A^β, giving general preference to the readings of the
latter. Against Charles, Stone (on the basis of his MS m) saw the shorter
Armenian Version (A^α) as of value primarily in filling lacunae in A^β. This
means, however, that while Burchard and Stone disagreed about the existence
of true recensions in the Armenian Version, they were not in disagreement
about the basic content of the version in its original form. Such is the case
because Burchard's eclectic method allowed him to use A^α-type MSS to fill
lacunae in the Armenian Version, while Stone's MS m does the same. What is
the original form of this version and hence of the ancient Greek MS from which
it was translated? It is similar to the so-called A^β; where A^β has lacunae vis-à-
vis Greek Group B, the best Armenian text fills these from the MSS composing
the so-called A^α, where possible.

Thus, Charles had used the Armenian Version to help eliminate Christian interpolations, but Burchard and Stone found that this version in its original form is similar to and only slightly less Christian than the critical text derived from Greek Group B. This supports the position of Hunkin and de Jonge.

Because the purpose of Anders Hultgård's dissertation[145] of 1971 was to determine the messianic beliefs of the Testaments in its original Jewish form by means (so far as possible) of text criticism, he devotes a significant first part of his study to textual matters and the conclusions of Charles, Hunkin, de Jonge, Burchard, and Stone.

To begin, he describes Mount Athos Laura MS 1403-K116, which he had been the first to photograph; according to Hultgård this MS is closely related but preferable to the known Mount Athos Laura MS 1132-148 (MS 1).[146] Then Hultgård examines the other Greek MSS of the Testaments. First, it is not clear to him why Charles preferred the Group A to the Group B MSS, except that perhaps, given Charles' assumption of an original Jewish Testaments, Group A with its various Christian omissions seemed nearer the original. He was wrong, however. The omissions and additions of Group A [MSS chi] are generally secondary and unsupported by the Armenian Version; Group A is of quite limited value.[147] Because even MSS chi do have occasionally superior readings, it may not be assumed however that these MSS have no value; therefore it is important to establish an accurate ranking within the Greek MSS.[148]

Second, in order to do this Hultgård analyzes short passages from each MS, drawing the following conclusions about the relationships between and relative superiority of the various Greek MSS:[149] first, MSS chi are a family but provide a generally corrupt witness to the Testaments; second, MSS bdgaefklm (Group B) have special relationships against MSS chi; third, MSS bdgklm are related by their longer readings in T Zebulun; fourth, MS e is independent but has special relationships to MSS af; fifth, MSS dlm are related as are MSS bk; and sixth, the Greek MSS in order of superiority are e, b, f, l, g. Thus, Hultgård maintains the existence of Groups A and B. Against Charles he prefers Group B. De Jonge's sub-Group γ (MSS aef) is partially correct since MS e is related to MSS af; but his sub-group δ (MSS bdg) does not exist because MS d forms a group with MSS lm. Moreover, the preference of Hunkin and de Jonge for MS b is incorrect because MS e is at least as valuable as MS b.[150]

Hultgård next evaluates the Armenian MSS, adding two more groups to the generally accepted Groups α and β. These he calls A^{mv} and A^Z after the MSS which make them up.[151] According to Hultgård, A^α is regularly inferior to A^β. Where it agrees with A^{mv} and A^Z against A^β, however, its readings are superior to A^β.[152] Concerning A^β itself he simply says that it has in the past been preferred and that most Armenian MSS witness its text including Stone's MSS nopqrt.[153] The third group, A^{mv}, is superior to A^β because it offers a more complete text than that provided by a conflation of A^α and A^β[154] And A^Z has very ancient, special readings.[155] Hultgård then indicates that special relationships exist between A^α and A^β; A^α and A^Z; A^Z and A^{mv}; A^{mv} and A^β.[156] However, A^Z and A^β have no such special relationships. Moreover, A^{zmv} are superior to $A^{\alpha\beta}$ and produce a text similar to MSS dg [so too Burchard] within Greek Group B. A^{zmv} may be used therefore to correct the Greek text of the Testaments.[157]

The main part of Hultgård's dissertation is not, however, the text-critical study. His primary purpose is to recover the original Jewish messianic passages within the Testaments on the assumption that this document was Jewish in its original form.[158] To give some idea of his methods and results, and particularly to show the use which he makes of his text-critical work, we provide here a description of his analysis of T Levi 4:2-6.[159] Hultgård first does a careful text-critical study of these verses[160] and gives a French translation of the resultant text.[161] The earliest text which can be reached by text-critical means is Christian: T Levi 4:2-6 describes the incarnation and crucifixion of Jesus.[162] Now, however, it is apparent to Hultgård that the original Jewish text had neither incarnation nor crucifixion; thus, when the incarnation materials are removed the text witnesses to the Jewish theme of God Himself coming to the world. That is, "il n'y a pas de doute que, dans le texte primitif, on attendait seulement la visite du Dieu car le terme ἐπισκέπτομαι s'emploie seulement en connexion avec Dieu."[163]

From the presentation itself, however, it is not clear on what grounds Hultgård reaches this conclusion. His grounds are not text-critical, nor are they explicitly literary-critical. It may be, therefore, that his conclusion is based simply on the assumption of the non-Christian origin of the Testaments. In any case, Hultgård's method is similar in each messianic passage discussed. Using these passages he reaches the following conclusions:[164] first, in most instances text criticism is not able to show that the Christian material in the Testaments is interpolated, although the pre-Christian text is usually easy to recognize. Second, the original messianic teaching of the Testaments is that God Himself visits His people; there may have been combined with this, however, a subordinate Davidic Messiah, which would support dating the Testaments ca. 175 B.C.E. Third, the Levi-Judah materials are Hasmonean and later, referring not to Messiahs but leaders of the people. Fourth, the unique element in the Testaments was the later addition (first century B.C.E.) of a priestly Messiah.

Thus, while Hultgård's study was not thoroughly text-critical insofar as he had to find other grounds on which to remove Christian interpolations, it is of particular interest in the present context because it affirmed to a large extent the text of the Testaments defended by Hunkin, de Jonge, Stone, and Burchard.

Burchard, in the introduction to his major article, had indicated that a re-evaluation of the Charles position on the Slavonic Version was needed. In 1970 this appeared in E. Turdeanu's extensive study of the MSS of that version.[165] It is his basic position that MS p is not (vs. Charles and Morfill) the best witness to this version.[166] After a comparison of texts from T Levi in the Slavonic MS a and the Greek MS Ff I.24 (b), Turdeanu concludes that MS a, relegated previously to a secondary place, is the primary witness to the longer Slavonic Version, being similar to de Jonge's sub-group γ.[167] The shorter Slavonic Version is, in Turdeanu's opinion, a recension of the longer[168] and betrays the tendency of adding anti-Semitic materials not present in the Greek MSS nor in the Slavonic MS a.[169]

From his analysis, Turdeanu reaches the following conclusions about the textual history of this version: first, it came into existence in the 12th century in the careful translation (like MS a) of a Greek MS similar to MSS aef (de Jonge's γ). Second, in the 13th century an anti-Semitic redaction (MS p) of this was made; and third, in the same century a shorter edition of this anti-Semitic redaction appeared.[170]

Closely related to the text-critical studies of Burchard, Stone, Hultgård and Turdeanu is that of Henk Jan de Jonge.[171] H. J. de Jonge's concern is to show the textual relationships principally among the Greek MSS of the Testaments, and he does this on the basis of a new collation of all of the Greek MSS (with the exception of MS h) for T Reuben, T Levi, T Zebulun, and T Benjamin.[172] Before discussing his methods and results, however, we should describe the state of research in the area of Greek MSS previous to the publication of this article. First, Charles had distinguished between MSS chi and MSS bdgaef, indicating that MSS chi (A) represented a better witness to the Testaments than MSS bdgaef (B), the longer Greek text.[173] Hunkin then argued in 1914 that, while these two MS groups existed, it was in fact MSS bdgaef which provided the better witness.[174] Similarly, in 1953[175] and more summarily in 1964,[176] M. de Jonge argued that Hunkin was correct in his preference for MSS kbdgaef[177] but that within these MSS distinctions were to be made, namely, MSS acf (called γ by de Jonge) and MSS kbdg (called δ by de Jonge) were separate groups with δ preferable to γ and MS b (within δ) preferable to MSS d and g. Then, in 1965-66, Burchard affirmed the superiority of MSS kbdgaef and added MS l to sub-group MSS kbdg.[178] Thus, when H. J. de Jonge wrote his article the existence of two major groups of MSS, Group A (MSS chi) and Group B (MSS lkbdgaef) had been affirmed; within these, B was superior and was itself composed of two sub-groups, δ (MSS lkbdg) and γ (MSS aef), of which δ was superior.

H. J. de Jonge's analysis of the MSS in terms of their dates, errors, and omissions led him, however, to some different conclusions about the nature of these groups.[179] In his study of the texts of T Reuben, T Levi, T Zebulun, and T Benjamin he finds that, except for secondary corruption, no one MS is dependent upon another.[180] The MSS are not, however, of equal value, but suffer to varying extents from omissions and other errors.[181] Moreover, while not dependent upon each other, individual MSS do show particular relationships to each other in terms of similar errors and omissions. On the basis of these relationships H. J. de Jonge establishes his schema. According to him, each individual MS or group of MSS with unique qualities derives from a separate archetype.[182] Specifically, there are six archetypes in the following descending order of value: bk, g, dlm, e, af, and chi.[183]

On the basis of these conclusions H. J. de Jonge states his results.[184] First, Group B does not exist. Those MSS considered a part of it (bkgldmeaf) have a split in transmission between MSS bk and the others; moreover, Group B includes within it the MSS òf Group A so that B is really representative of ω, the archetype of the whole tradition. Second, Group A is "little more than a late and free re-working of an MS of the text type designated by B."[185] Third, M. de Jonge's γ and δ do not exist. Fourth, MS b and MS g do not have the same archetype; rather, fifth, there is an archetype of the tradition (ω) which "eventually decays into the archetype of Group A."[186] That is, the present MSS depend upon various archetypes, each of which shows a stage in the development of the textual tradition. MSS bk stem from the "*hyparchtypus*" from which developed the archetypes of MS g, then MSS ldm, e, and af. The latest and poorest was the basis of the texts in Charles' Group A (MSS chi).

It is clear, therefore, that in H. J. de Jonge's analysis significant changes have been proposed in the make-up of the various groups which compose the Greek textual tradition. That is, his analysis denies the existence of Group B and of sub-groups γ and δ, while at the same time organizing the MSS under six archetypes. In terms of the actual effect on the textual criticism of the Testaments, however, it should be noted that his study reaches the same major conclusion as was arrived at by Hunkin, M. de Jonge, Burchard, and Hultgård on the basis of the Greek MSS and by Burchard, Stone, Hultgård, and Turdeanu on the basis of the Armenian and Slavonic Versions. That is, the longer "Christian" text of the Testaments receives a primary place in text criticism while the shorter is relegated to a secondary position.

We have made a slight diversion in order to be able to consider the major text-critical studies of recent years together. Not since Hunkin and Messel, fifty years before, had such studies been made. These two scholars wrote in reaction to men such as Conybeare, Bousset, Preuschen, and Charles. Some indication, therefore, of the little work done on the text criticism of the Testaments is shown by the fact that Charles is still the main opponent of Burchard, Stone, Hultgård, Turdeanu, and H. J. de Jonge. They repudiate important text-critical opinions regarded practically sacrosanct by scholarship for more than fifty years.

Again, the Origins of the Testaments

As indicated already, the volume which contained Burchard's study also held two further discussions of the Testaments. Both of these deal directly with the question of its origin and should now be considered.

J. Jervell[187] tried to determine the type of Christian who interpolated this originally Jewish writing.[188] To do this Jervell first considers the universalism of the Testaments.[189] He rejects Philonenko's claim that such universalism appears in Qumran and denies it but a very minor role in the Judaism of the period. This doctrine is, therefore, a Christian interpolation.[190]

Jervell next reads the Testaments through the eyes of this universalism-minded interpolator and so establishes the following propositions: first, the interpolator is interested not in the ethical paraenesis of the Testaments but in its prophecy; second, he alters this prophecy in order to teach that a) Gentiles shall have a place in salvation, b) Jews have opposed the Messiah, c) but may be saved by obedience to the new Lawgiver-Messiah; third, he writes at a time when the salvation of the Gentiles is no longer problematic but that of the Jews is.[191] According to Jervell, the prophecies of the original Testaments concerned the future of Israel.[192] The interpolator has changed this by adding salvation for the Gentiles and promising it to the Jews through obedience to Christ.[193] Thus, the interpolator's purpose is to insure his readers of the future salvation of Israel even after its rejection of Christ.[194] Related to this also is the Jesus-Lawgiver motif. The Jews (specifically not the Gentiles) will be saved as they become obedient to him and his law.[195]

When might this redaction-interpolation have taken place? The terminus post quem is 70 C.E., since the destruction of the Temple is clearly referred to by the interpolator.[196] The terminus ad quem is less definite but *before* 100 C.E., because first, the motif of the Church as the New Israel has not appeared; second, the traditions of the Testaments are Jewish-Christian but not of the later heretical type; third, salvation of the Jews is a major concern and one that disappeared early from the Church; and fourth, the christology of the Testaments (Jesus as Lawgiver) is early and Jewish-Christian.[197] Concerning the elements of a higher christology which he finds elsewhere in the Testaments, Jervell concludes that this must be the work of a second and later Christian interpolator.[198]

Jervell's study is in many ways similar to that of Philonenko. They both operated on the assumption that the original Testaments was a Jewish document,[199] and they disregarded questions concerning this original document, working rather with those materials in the Testaments usually thought of as Christian.[200] Although Philonenko and Jervell came to rather opposite conclusions about the origin of these materials, they stood on the same unique ground in their attempt to work on the Testaments from the perspective of its interpolations.

The same volume contained another article concerned with the origins of the Testaments. Like Jervell and Philonenko, J. Thomas[201] assumes the Jewish origin of the Testaments; but unlike them, his purpose is to discover the *Sitz im Leben* of the original document.

After discussing the relationship between paraenesis and apocalyptic and their compatibility within the Testaments,[202] Thomas argues that the Testaments is the product of pre-Maccabean Judaism.[203] This discussion focuses on three topics: Levi-rule as a probable Qumran interpolation; T Levi 8-13 and its parallels in the Qumran Aramaic Levi fragments; historical allusions.

Concerning Levi-rule as a probable Qumran interpolation, Thomas recalls the position of R. H. Charles that the Testaments originated in the early Hasmonean period during the height of popularity of the Levi-Maccabean line, but was interpolated in an anti-Levi manner as the later Maccabeans proved themselves more and more corrupt.[204] In agreement with Charles, Thomas argues that the anti-levitical materials in the Testaments would not have been added in the early Hasmonean period.[205] In opposition to Charles, however, he is of the opinion that it is not these but rather the pro-Levi materials which are the interpolations. To substantiate his position Thomas repeats the results of Schnapp's work on T Levi 2:3—6:2. This section which elevates Levi literally to the heavens is, according to Schnapp, an interpolation. Preceding and following it is the condemnation of Levi for his destruction of Shechem, a condemnation paralleled for most of the Patriarchs within the Testaments. However, in T Levi 5:3 God's angel gives to Levi a sword for his deed; thus T Levi 2:3—6:2 with its pro-levitical tendency breaks into an otherwise integral story, contradicts its condemnation of Levi, and so destroys the parallels with the other Patriarchs. The pro-levitical tendency is, therefore, an interpolation and may not be used to place the original Testaments in the early Hasmonean period.[206] By whom, then, was the Testaments interpolated so as to put the sword in the hands of the levitical priesthood? Thomas believes that this was done within the Qumran Community or, possibly, by supporters of the warring high priesthood.[207]

Concerning the second of the topics related to the time of writing of the Testaments, T Levi 8—13 and the parallel Qumran Aramaic fragments, Thomas seeks to show that T Levi 8—9, 11—13 is an interpolation from a source used by these fragments.[208] First, T Levi 8—13 is interpolated because its materials are unlike those in the rest of the Testaments, with T Levi 9 on the cultic law unique to the document. Second, T Levi 8—9, 11—13 is quite different from the Aramaic fragments, but contains the same story; T Levi 10, however, speaks of the sins of the tribe of Levi and is not present in the Aramaic fragments. Third, the Testaments was not produced at Qumran because that community was cult-oriented and shows no signs of having used the Testaments. This means, therefore, that T Levi 8—9, 11—13 is a pro-Levi, pro-cultic addition interpolated around the more typical T Levi 10 by someone from the "priestly circles of Palestine."[209]

Thus, in his discussion of the first two topics Thomas attempted to show that the motif of the exaltation-perfection of Levi in the Testaments does not stem from the original writer but from an interpolator who wanted to set Levi in a special light above the rest of his brothers.

Thomas' third concern is the dating of the original Testaments on the basis of historical allusions within it. First, from his discussion of the integrity of the anti-Levi material, he concludes that the Testaments cannot be the product of the earlier Maccabean-Hasmonean period. It comes rather from the time of Jason and Menelaus when the priesthood was in disrepute.[210] Second, Thomas repeats Bickerman's statement that the coins mentioned in T Jos

16:4-5 were used before 285 B.C.E. and shortly after 200 B.C.E. He agrees with Bickerman that the period from 200-150 B.C.E. is when the Testaments was written, because a date prior to 285 B.C.E. is too early. More exactly, since there is no reference in the Testaments to Antiochus IV (with the possible exception of T Sim 6:3-4), he concludes that it was written between 200 and 175 B.C.E.[211]

Thomas next examines the figures of Joseph, Levi, and Judah in the Testaments in order to show that they are contemporary Jewish symbols in the world in which this document was written. It is Joseph who is the central character in the Testaments.[212] He alone among the Patriarchs merits the double narration of his life,[213] and it is he who is the exemplification of the two main paraenetical themes, i.e., the love of God and universal neighbor-love.[214] Of what is Joseph a symbol? He represents Egyptian diaspora Judaism.[215] Thomas argues that the Jews lived in a world of such collective symbols by which those people under a particular symbol were exhorted to assume their genuine being ("was dein wahres Wesen ist").[216] Although Joseph was a symbol for various collectives, Thomas says (on the basis of T Naph 5—7) that the more joyful situation of Joseph denotes a part of Judaism relatively unbothered by the miseries of the homeland. This part is probably the Egyptian Diaspora.[217] Then, on the basis of this identification, Thomas concludes that the Testaments is a letter to the Jews of Egypt commanding them to be like their symbol, the pure Joseph.[218]

The other two symbols, Judah and Levi, are dealt with much more briefly. Judah serves "as an apocalyptic symbol for the leadership task of Palestinian Judaism."[219] That is, for the Egyptian Jews, Judah serves as the symbol of the Palestinian heart of Judaism and the messianic hope centered there for all Israel. Judah does not represent any present political figure.[220] Nor does Levi; he is a symbol, neither positive nor negative, of Judaism's priestly families.[221] Specifically, he symbolizes the right of the priesthood to interpret and declare the Law.[222]

Given the above, Thomas then explains the purpose of the writer of the Testaments: he writes from Palestine to his fellow Jews in Egypt, calling upon them as the faithful Joseph's people to remain within the community of Judah and Levi and to avoid the gods and vices of Egypt.[223] With this purpose in mind, Thomas' final section raises the question of the form of the original Testaments.[224] Finding no clear indication that this is the covenant formula (Bundesformular) suggested by Baltzer,[225] Thomas takes up a study by C. Andresen which, using Christian texts primarily, had shown the existence of a Diasporasendschreiben form.[226] According to Thomas this could have existed by 200 B.C.E. Because of many similarities between it and the Testaments in terms of personal speech, authoritarianism, and the people-God-faith complex, Thomas concludes that the Diasporasendschreiben is the best way to explain the overall composition of the Testaments.[227]

The volume which contained the articles by Burchard, Jervell, and Thomas presents no consensus concerning the origin of the Testaments. While

Burchard was working on the analysis of the text-critical theories of Charles, theories very important for the question of origins, Jervell and Thomas were operating on the assumption of the existence of an originally Jewish Testaments with little regard for the work of de Jonge and those who supported him. That is, both Jervell and Thomas suppose a certain body of Christian interpolations and go on from there, either using that body exclusively (Jervell) or not at all (Thomas). Such a supposition is justified, however, only from a Schnapp-Charles perspective, i.e., a perspective which feels confident in distinguishing between Jewish and Christian teaching. To this extent both Jervell and Thomas belong in the period between 1908 and 1951 and show the lasting influence of Charles.[228]

Something similar may also be said of P. W. Macky's dissertation of 1969.[229] It is his purpose to seek the date of writing of the original Testaments on the basis of a comparison of its theology with that of the Old and New Testament, Jubilees, I Enoch, other pseudepigraphical writings, rabbinic writings, Philo, the Church Fathers, and the Qumran literature.[230] Given the fairly sure dates of writing of these documents, e.g., Jubilees and I Enoch 6-36, 83-90 — late 2nd century B.C.E.; I Enoch 37-71 — 50 B.C.E. to 50 C.E.; Qumran — 175 to 40 B.C.E.,[231] Macky argues that it is only necessary to discover which of these have the most theological parallels with the Testaments in order to determine its date of composition. The lengthy body of the dissertation then follows with chapters devoted to "Heavenly Kingdom: God," "Supernatural Mediators," "Kingdom of the Enemy," "Levi and Judah," "Levi and the New Priest," and "The Branch and God's Appearing." In each chapter Macky first describes the teaching of the Testaments and then offers parallels from the literature mentioned above, although he already noted that the most parallels are to be expected from Qumran and the New Testament.[232]

Macky's dissertation is too long to summarize in full, but to make clear his method and results, we may give a description of Chapter 3, "Supernatural Mediators."[233] After an analysis of the teaching of the Testaments on angels and good spirits,[234] Macky discusses parallel teachings in his other literature.[235] The following are his major observations: first, the punishing angels of T Levi 3 have parallels in Jubilees, I Enoch, and the Qumran literature; therefore, the angelology of the Testaments represents the early Jewish teaching. What of the seven heavens of T Levi 3? Such a teaching appears in Judaism only after the advent of Christianity; but in the Testaments it is an interpolation.[236] Second, angels as God's messengers appear in all periods of Judaism (and Christianity) and give no clue for dating the Testaments.[237] Third, the angel fighting within man in the Testaments appears only in the Qumran literature.[238] Then he turns to parallels with the teachings of the Testaments on good spirits and makes the following observations: first, spiritual dualism like that of the Testaments made its original appearance in the Qumran literature;[239] second, the theme of the present activity of God's Spirit has its best parallels within the NT.[240] On the basis of these parallels Macky concludes that the Qumran literature has the best parallels to the Testaments and, along with Jubilees and I Enoch, indicates that it is a product of the first century B.C.E.[241]

In the same way Macky analyzes each of his theological themes and, in a brief final section of his dissertation, brings together his results. First, the Testaments was originally written in the first century B.C.E., probably somewhat after the taking of Jerusalem in 63 B.C.E. by Pompey. Second, it was not written nor used by the Qumran Community, since it reveals sharp theological contrasts with that community and has not been found among the community's documents. Third, therefore, the Testaments arose within the Judaism represented by such pseudepigraphal writings as Jubilees, I Enoch, and the Psalms of Solomon.[242]

Macky's dissertation is an extensive work of much value in bringing together various theological themes in the Testaments with their parallels in the literature relatively contemporary with the Testaments. As indicated in introducing his study, however, the work of Macky belongs in many ways to the period in Testaments study between 1908 and 1951, when the Jewish origin of the document and easy detection of Christian additions was assumed. Thus, for example, already in 1905 R. H. Charles[243] had argued that the parallels between the Testaments and Jubilees required the dating of the Testaments with Jubilees ca. 105 B.C.E. To this extent, then, not only Jervell and Thomas but also Macky show the lasting influence of Charles right to the present.

Shortly after Macky had completed his study, J. Becker's literary-critical analysis of the Testaments was published.[244] Although text-, source-, and form-critical considerations are not absent from this study, it is particularly interesting in that it affirms the position taken by Schnapp in 1884 that only literary criticism can resolve the problem of the development of the Testaments into its present form.[245] Unlike Schnapp, however, who had found three layers of development in the document, Becker finds many more and so carries his predecessor's method to a highly complex conclusion. It is fitting, therefore, that this verse-for-verse search for individual and more integrated additions to the Testaments should be our last contribution to the complex history of research on a most intriguing and, as the history shows, ambiguous document.

Becker begins his analysis with an examination of the Greek and Armenian MSS of the Testaments. He agrees that the Greek Group B MSS are superior to those of Group A, but says also that this latter group should receive more weight than presently given it.[246] Likewise, he says that the Armenian Version must be given a more nearly equal consideration with Greek A and B than de Jonge had said.[247]

Becker next discusses possible sources used by the Testaments and finds, contrary to de Jonge, that T Levi uses no written sources but only oral tradition.[248] Similarly, he argues that the Hebrew T Naphtali is later than that of the Testaments and of no use source-critically.[249]

In tracing the history of research[250] beginning with Schnapp, Becker criticizes de Jonge by asking six questions. Why is the clearly Christian material of the Testaments apparent only in the sections on the future? How could a Christian ca. 200 C.E. use Jewish traditions so easily? Why does the Christian material have the appearance of interpolation? Is everything that de Jonge describes as Christian really Christian? Why does de Jonge depend so heavily on MS b and fail to see the long tradition history? Why does the Christian writer introduce doublets into his text?[251] Within the same history Becker then states eleven reasons why the Testaments cannot come directly from Qumran.[252] In this way he rejects Philonenko's position in order to be able to concentrate on his major opponent, de Jonge.[253] At this point he makes his method clear: text criticism is not able to remove the Christian materials from the Testaments and it is necessary, therefore, to return to literary criticism to do this.[254]

Before beginning his literary-critical study of the individual testaments, Becker makes important preliminary observations. First, the present framework of the Testaments is Semitic Greek and not Hebrew;[255] second, the Sin-Exile-Return pattern contains no apocalyptic, dualism, nor messianism;[256] third, the Levi-Judah pattern has no dualism nor messianism except where a Christian hand is at work.[257]

A description of the whole of Becker's analysis of the Testaments would be far too lengthy here. In order to make clear his method and results, however, we shall discuss in detail his analysis of the first of the farewell speeches (*Abschiedsreden*) of the Testaments, T Reuben.[258] He begins with a discussion of its first block of material, T Reuben 1:5-10, in which Reuben's sin of fornication is the theme. According to Becker this same theme appears in a parallel account in T Reuben 3:9—4:5.[259] There are important differences, however, between the two accounts.[260] In T Reuben 1:6-10 the emphasis is upon the fact of Reuben's sin, whereas in the second account it is upon the "psychological background" with its attendant attention to the detail of the sinning. In T Reuben 1:6-10 the paraenetical command is "do not sin," whereas in T Reuben 3:9—4:5 it is "avoid the causes of sin."

Given these differences, Becker next seeks the form of T Reuben 3:9-15 and finds in it elements of the Hellenistic novel with its psychological, erotic interests coupled with Jewish paraenesis.[261] Then in T Reuben 4:1-5 he finds Hellenistic Jewish motifs and concludes that T Reuben 3:9—4:5 is the product of Hellenistic Judaism.[262] Concerning T Reuben 1:3-10 he says simply that it gives a picture of the Palestinian Jewish world,[263] but its language is a Semitic Greek (*semitisierendes Griechisch*).[264] Because T Reuben 1:3-10 and 3:9—4:5 have few similarities, they stem from different authors; T Reuben 3:9—4:5 is a secondary addition to the *Grundstock* 1:3-10.[265]

Given this literary-critical evidence that T Reuben is not a unity, Becker discusses T Reuben 2:1—3:8.[266] It is no unity because between T Reuben 2:2 and 2:3 there is a break in the text, and T Reuben 3:1 and 3:7 are doublets.[267]

Specifically, T Reuben 2:1-2/3:3-8 belong together on the theme of the seven evil spirits. However, T Reuben 2:3—3:2 breaks into this with a list of neutral/anthropological spirits. Therefore, the inserted section T Reuben 2:3—3:2 is an interpolation.[268] Nonetheless, T Reuben 2:1-2/3:3-8 is also an interpolation, but in the original document.[269] This is so because only T Reuben 3:3 has any relationship whatsoever to the genuine T Reuben 1:3-10. The rest of T Reuben 2:1-2/3:3-8 (especially its interest in the theme of evil spirits) has little in common with the themes of the original Testaments.

Having already discussed T Reuben 3:9—4:5 as his justification for a literary-critical search for disunity within T Reuben, Becker next discusses T Reuben 4:6—6:4.[270] This is a separate section because T Reuben 4:5 and 4:6 have a break between them and T Reuben 6:4 clearly ends the section.[271] It is a literary unit without internal suture,[272] unrelated to the previous material: first, its primary figure is Joseph, so it does not connect well with the original T Reuben 1:3-10; second, the psychological element of T Reuben 3:9—4:5 is absent from it.[273] Against Charles, the original language of this unit is a semitized Greek, and its form is that defined by H. Thyen as the synagogue homily of the Jewish-Hellenistic Diaspora.[274]

Becker then considers T Reuben 6:5-12, the last section of that testament. The material present here is to be found in all of the Testaments, so that all end on an eschatological note. This material is also, however, the most complex of the Testaments.[275]

First, T Reuben 6:5-12 has no relationship to T Reuben 4:6—6:4, but is not a unity either. It has four separate parts, T Reuben 6:5-7, 6:8, 6:9, 6:10-12.[276] That 6:5-7 is a unity can be shown from a similar structure in T Sim 5:4-6 and T Dan 5:4. It is a Jewish text, since no Christian would be concerned with jealousy toward Levi; but it cannot be shown that a Semitic text underlies this unit.[277]

T Reuben 6:8 does not belong to the previous verses, because it makes no mention of disobedience to Levi. It is in fact the first Christian interpolation in T Reuben. Why? First, the singular use of "highpriest" in the verse appears also in T Sim 7:2 where the Christian reference is clear. Second, the use of "Christ" is paralleled in T Levi 10:2 and T Asher 7:2 where it has a Christian significance.[278]

T Reuben 6:9 is, however, unrelated to 6:8. According to Becker, this neighbor-love motif is a theme of the original Testaments and belongs to it.[279] Therefore, this verse serves as a clue in resolving the question of the originality of T Reuben 6:5-8. Because these verses and T Reuben 6:10-12 are doublets on Levi-Judah, one is unnecessary; and since the genuine Levi-Judah materials in the Testaments come after the last paraenesis, T Reuben 6:5-8 is secondary.[280]

Becker next analyzes T Reuben 6:10-12 on the assumption that as a whole it is a part of the original document.[281] First, T Reuben 6:12 is a Christian text because of its reference to invisible battles fought by and sufferings of the Messiah.[282] T Reuben 6:11b is, however, in the best MSS (Greek Group A and the Armenian Version) a Jewish text. Its Semitic Greek, not present in the Christian interpolations, is a secondary proof of its Jewish origin; and T Reuben 6:10-11a is also Jewish since it is Levi who blesses Israel and Judah.[283]

At this point Becker brings together his conclusions about the development of the Testament of Reuben. The present testament has the following outline:

1. life history	1:3-10
2. spirits	2:1—3:8
3. life history and paraenesis	3:9—4:5
4. paraenesis	4:6—6:4
5. future and paraenesis	6:5-12

Of this material, the following belongs to the original document:

1. introduction and beginning of teaching	1:3-5
2. life history	1:6-10
3. paraenesis	6:9
4. Levi-Judah	6:10-12

This means that between T Reuben 1:10 and 6:9 many complexes of materials have been added from one or more redactors.[284]

After similar analysis of each of the testaments Becker states his conclusions about the document as a whole. In its present form the Testaments is composed of three levels of material: first, a Hellenistic-Jewish original composed primarily of moral exhortation; second, a Hellenistic-Jewish enlargement of this including synagogue-homily, additional Levi-Judah and Sin-Exile-Return, dualistic, apocalyptic, and messianic materials; third, a series of Christian additions. The second and third levels were added by various people over a long period.[285]

Concerning place and date of writing of the original Testaments Becker says that the former is definitely not Palestine because of the poor knowledge of Palestinian geography exhibited by the writer. Egypt may, therefore, be the place of writing.[286] As to date, it is pre-70 B.C.E. because the Romans do not yet appear as rulers; a probable date, based upon T Naph 5:8, is ca. 220 B.C.E. as the Syrians enter Palestine to rule. The Jewish interpolations then make their appearance in the Testaments between 220 B.C.E. and about 100 C.E.[287]

It should be clear that Becker's main tool was literary criticism with a generally secondary use of textual criticism. He viewed the original Testaments as a work of moral exhortation without elements of dualism, spirits, and the like which in recent study have been associated with Qumran. Becker indicated, however, against Dupont-Sommer, that the interpolations in the Testaments cannot come directly from Qumran since many of these are contrary to that community's teaching and both Jewish levels of materials in the Testaments are Hellenistic and not Palestinian.

FOOTNOTES

[1] Marc Philonenko, *Les interpolations chrétiennes des Testaments des Douze Patriarches et les manuscrits de Qoumrân* (Paris: Presses universitaires de France, 1960) 3. The book appeared originally under the same title in *RHPR* 38 (1958) 309-43; 39 (1959) 14-38. Our pagination follows that of the book.

[2] Ibid., 3.

[3] Ibid., 4-6.

[4] Ibid.

[5] Ibid., 7.

[6] These include such texts as T Levi 16:3-6 (p. 13), T Benj 9:3-5 (p. 22), T Benj 10:7-8 (p. 31), and T Dan 5:13 (pp. 34-35). All produce nearly the same uniform result, i.e., the reference is to the Teacher and not Jesus.

[7] Philonenko, *Les interpolations chrétiennes* 59-60: "*Les Testaments des Douze Patriarches* nous ont été transmis avec une remarquable fidélité et, tels que nous les connaissons par la tradition grecque, ils sont libres de toute interpolation chrétienne de quelque importance. . . . Mais ces vieux textes esséniens, maintenant réhabilités, peuvent et doivent, au même titre que la *Règle,* les *Hôdâyôt* ou *l'Écrit de Damas,* être utilisés pour mieux connaître l'histoire et les doctrines de la secte juive." "The Testaments of the Twelve Patriarchs have been passed on to us with remarkable faithfulness and, such as we know them through the Greek tradition, are free of any important Christian interpolations. . . . But these ancient Essene texts, now rehabilitated, can and should (like the Rule, the Thanksgiving Hymns and the Damascus Document) be used in order to better understand the history and doctrines of the Jewish sect."

[8] J. Liver, "The Doctrine of the Two Messiahs in Sectarian Literature in the Time of the Second Commonwealth," *HTR* 52 (1959) 149-85.

[9] Ibid., 151-56.

[10] Ibid., 156-63.

[11] Ibid., 165.

[12] Ibid., 166-77.

[13] Ibid., 178.

[14] Ibid., 180.

[15] Ibid., 181.

[16] Ibid., 182.

[17] Ibid., 184.

[18] Ibid., 183.

[19] Ibid., 183, 149.

[20] M. de Jonge, "Christian Influence in the Testaments of the Twelve Patriarchs," *NovT* 4 (1960) 182-235.

[21] Ibid., 184, 186.

[22] Ibid.

[23] Ibid., 185, 187-88.

[24] Ibid., 185, 186.

[25] Ibid., 189.

[26] Ibid.

[27] Ibid.

[28] Ibid., 190.

[29] Ibid., 191-99.

[30] Ibid., 197.

[31] Ibid., 200-205.

[32] Ibid., 205.

[33] Ibid., 217-18.

[34] F.-M. Braun, "Les Testaments des XII Patriarches et le problème de leur origine," *RB* 67 (1960) 516-49.

[35]Ibid., 522-28.

[36]Ibid., 528.

[37]Ibid., 530.

[38]Ibid., 530-33.

[39]Ibid., 539-40.

[40]Ibid., 540-41.

[41]Ibid., 535-43.

[42]Ibid., 545.

[43]Ibid.

[44]Ibid., 546.

[45]Ibid., 546-48.

[46]Ibid., 548. Four years later Braun (*Jean le théologien: les grandes traditions d'Israël et l'accord des écritures selon le Quatrième Évangile* [Paris: Librarie Lecoffre, 1964] 233-51) reconsidered the question of the origin of the Testaments in defense of his use of it as a witness to "le bas-Judaïsme." His primary conclusion concerning the Jewish diaspora origin of the Testaments was like that of 1960. But significant differences appeared in his evaluation of individual elements of Testaments traditions: 1) whereas in 1960 he had argued that concern for the Law could not be Christian, he now said that this concern could be as easily Jewish-Christian as Jewish; 2) whereas he had argued that God-neighbor love might have a Jewish origin, he now said it was Christian; 3) whereas he had said that the Christian materials were superficial in the Testaments he now indicated that certain of these (Jesus as Lawgiver, Levi 18, Judah 21) were integrated into the text of the document.

[47]P. Geoltrain, rev. of M. Philonenko, *Les interpolations*, *RHPR* 41 (1961) 224-26.

[48]M.-E. Boismard, rev. of M. Philonenko, *Les interpolations*, *RB* 68 (1961) 419-23.

[49]P. Wernberg-Møller, rev. of M. Philonenko, *Les interpolations*, *JSS* 6 (1961) 292-93.

[50]G. Bernini, rev. of M. Philonenko, *Les interpolations*, *Greg* 43 (1962) 335-37.

[51]G. Delling, rev. of M. Philonenko, *Les interpolations*, *OLZ* 57 (1962) 48-50.

[52]L. Rost, "Testamente der XII Patriarchen," *RGG*³ 6 (1962) 701-02.

[53]Ibid., 702.

[54]M. Smith, "The Testaments of the Twelve Patriarchs," *IDB* 4 (1962) 575-79. Pierre Grelot ("Le messie dans les apocryphes de l'Ancien Testament. État de la question," *RechBib* 6 [1962] 33-41) discussed the priestly Messiah, indicating that this figure appears only in the Qumran literature and the Testaments. While according to Grelot the original Testaments contained a doctrine of two Messiahs like that of Qumran, the present Testaments is a Christian adaptation in which the two separate Messiahs of the original document have been amalgamated into the one person, Jesus.

[55]M. de Jonge, "Once More: Christian Influence in the Testaments of the Twelve Patriarchs," *NovT* 5 (1962) 311-19.

[56]Ibid., 312.

[57]Ibid.

[58]Ibid., 313, 317.

[59]Ibid., 314.

[60]Bruce Vawter, "Levitical Messianism and the New Testament," *The Bible in Current Catholic Thought* (ed. John L. McKenzie; New York: Herder and Herder, 1962) 83-99.

[61]Ibid., 86, 89, 91, 94-97.

[62]Ibid., 93.

[63]Ibid., 90-92.

[64]Roger Le Déaut, "Le titre de Summus Sacerdos donné a Melchisedech est-il d'origine juive?" *RSR* 50 (1962) 222-29.

[65]Ibid., 222.

[66]Ibid., 223-25.

[67]Ibid., 228.

[68]Le Déaut does not say this specifically but it is implied on p. 228, where he finds that of Jewish and Christian sources it is Hebrews, Ambrose, the Apostolic Constitutions, and T Levi 3:5-6 which offer closest parallels on the *Summus Sacerdos*.

[69]Joachim Gnilka, "Der Hymnus des Zacharias," *BZ* 6 (1962) 215-38.

[70]Ibid., 229.

[71]Ibid., 235.

[72]Ibid., 236-37.

[73]Ibid., 237.

[74]Ibid., 237-38.

[75]Joachim Gnilka, "2 Kor 6,14-7,1 im Lichte der Qumranschriften und der Zwölf-Patriarchen-Testamente," *Neutestamentliche Aufsätze: Festschrift für Prof. Josef Schmid zum 70. Geburtstag* (eds. J. Blinzler, O. Kuss, and F. Mussner; Regensburg: F. Pustet, 1963) 86-99.

[76]Ibid., 94-95. Gnilka does not find this in the Testaments.

[77]Ibid., 96-97.

[78]Ibid., 98.

[79]Martin Rese, "Überprüfung einiger Thesen von Joachim Jeremias zum Thema des Gottesknechtes im Judentum," *ZTK* 60 (1963) 24. This is in response to Joachim Jeremias, "Παῖς θεοῦ im Spätjudentum in der Zeit nach der Entstehung der LXX," *TWNT* 5 (1954) 676-98.

[80]G. Widengren, "Royal Ideology and the Testaments of the Twelve Patriarchs," *Promise and Fulfillment: Essays Presented to Professor S. H. Hooke in Celebration of His Ninetieth Birthday, 21st January 1964, by Members of the Society for Old Testament Study and Others* (ed. F. F. Bruce; Edinburgh: T. and T. Clark, 1963) 202-12.

[81]Klaus Baltzer, *Das Bundesformular* (Neukirchen-Vluyn: Neukirchener Verlag,[2] 1964).

[82]Ibid., 147-48. A second form-critical study related to the Testaments in this period is that of Odil Hannes Steck (*Israel und das gewaltsame Geschick der Propheten: Untersuchungen zur Überlieferung des deuteronomistischen Geschichtsbildes im Alten Testament, Spätjudentum und Urchristentum* (Neukirchen-Vluyn: Neukirchener Verlag, 1967). Like Baltzer, Steck assumed the Jewish origin of the Testaments and found in its Sin-Exile-Return passages (pp. 149-53) elements of the "deuteronomistischen Geschichtsbildes." According to Steck (pp. 184-89) this is a Palestinian form found in the OT, Pseudepigrapha, and parts of the Gospel tradition.

[83]Ibid., 103, 148-58.

[84]Ibid., 158.

[85]At this point we should mention Otto Eissfeldt (*Einleitung in das Alte Testament* [Tübingen: J. C. B. Mohr[3] 1964] 855-62) who said that with the work of Otzen and Milik the Qumran origin of the Testaments was made probable.

[86]M. de Jonge (ed.), *Testamenta XII Patriarcharum Edited according to Cambridge University Library MS Ff I.24 fol. 203a-262b with Short Notes* (Leiden: E. J. Brill, 1964). A second edition appeared in 1970.

[87]Chr. Burchard, rev. of M. de Jonge (ed.), *Testamenta XII Patriarcharum*, *RQ* 5 (1965) 281-84.

[88]Christoph Burchard, "Neues zur Überlieferung der Testamente der zwölf Patriarchen," *NTS* 12 (1965-1966) 245-58.

[89]Christoph Burchard, "Das Lamm in der Waagschale," *ZNW* 57 (1966) 219-28.

[90]Klaus Koch, "Das Lamm, das Ägypten vernichtet," *ZNW* 57 (1966) 79-93.

[91]Joachim Jeremias, "Das Lamm, das aus der Jungfrau hervorging: Test. Jos. 19:8," *ZNW* 57 (1966) 217.

[92]Ibid., 218.

[93]Burchard, "Das Lamm," 220.

[94]A. J. B. Higgins, "The Priestly Messiah," *NTS* 13 (1966-1967) 211-39.

[95]Ibid., 211-19.

[96]Ibid., 223.

[97]Ibid., 223-28.

[98]Ibid., 229-30.

[99]R. A. Stewart, "The Sinless High Priest," *NTS* 14 (1967-1968) 126-35.

[100]Ibid., 126.

[101]Ibid., 127.

[102]Ibid., 129.

[103]Ibid.

[104]Ibid., 131-34.

[105]Ibid., 130.

[106]Ibid., 128-29.

[107]Ibid., 135.

[108]Christoph Burchard, "Zur armenischen Überlieferung der Testamente der zwölf Patriarchen," *Studien zu den Testamenten der zwölf Patriarchen* (ed. Walther Eltester; Berlin: Töpelmann, 1969) 1-29.

[109]Ibid., 1-4.

[110]Ibid., 4.

[111]Ibid., 6-13.

[112]Ibid., 13-15.

[113]This period (500-700 C.E.), considered the high point of classical Armenian literature, followed upon Mesrop's development of the Armenian alphabet and was marked by the translation of the Bible. Preuschen assumed that the Testaments was translated from Greek during this period. Such has become the common opinion although, so far as I am aware, there is no direct evidence to substantiate it.

[114]Burchard, "Zur armenischen Überlieferung," 15-27.

[115]Ibid., 15.

[116]Ibid., 16.

[117]Ibid.

[118]Ibid.

[119]Here the superscriptions indicate the particular Armenian MSS used by Charles.

[120]Burchard, "Zur armenischen Überlieferung," 16, 22.

[121]Ibid., 20, 22.

[122]Ibid.

[123]Ibid., 20-22.

[124]Ibid., 22.

[125]Ibid., 17.

[126]Ibid., 16, 17.

[127]Ibid., 23.

[128]Ibid., 24.

[129]Ibid.

[130]Ibid.

[131]Ibid., 24-25.

[132]Ibid., 25-27.

[133]Ibid., 27. He says, "Er [Charles] behandelte die armenische Version als mechanische Übersetzung einer eigenwilligen, inbesonders von christlichen Interpolationen relativ freien Vorlage, sie ist aber die stellenweise freie und kürzende Wiedergabe eines Textes, der von seinen engeren Verwandten [Greek MSS] bdghl nicht weit abstand." "He treated the Armenian Version as the mechanical translation of an independent *Vorlage* relatively free of Christian interpolations. It is however the partially free and abbreviating repetition of a text which did not stand far away from its close relatives bdghl."

[134]Ibid., 28.

[135]Michael E. Stone, *The Testament of Levi: A First Study of the Armenian MSS of the Testaments of the XII Patriarchs in the Convent of St. James, Jerusalem, with Text, Critical Apparatus, Notes and Translation* (Jerusalem: St. James Press, 1969) 3.

[136]Ibid., 22.

[137]Ibid., 27.

[138]Ibid.

[139]Ibid., 28.

[140]Ibid., 28-29.

[141]Ibid., 29.

[142]Ibid., 29-30.

[143]Ibid., 42.

[144]Ibid., 44.

[145]Anders Hultgård, *Croyances messianiques des Test. XII Patr.: critique textuelle et commentaire des passages messianiques* (Uppsala: Skriv Service AB, 1971).

[146]Ibid., 3-4.

[147]Ibid., 4-6.

[148]Ibid., 8.

[149]Ibid., 21.

[150]See pp. 73-74 of this study for the evaluation of MS e by Henk Jan de Jonge. The strong differences may be explained by Hultgård's use of a very limited number of verses in the establishment of his schema. They do agree, however, in separating MS e from MSS af.

[151]Hultgård, *Croyances messianiques des Test. XII Patr.* 25. MS m is the text preferred by Stone; MSS vz are respectively Burchard's Erewan 353 and 1500.

[152]Ibid., 30.

[153]Ibid., 31.

[154]Ibid., 32-33.

[155]Ibid., 33.

[156]Ibid., 35-37.

[157]Ibid.

[158]Ibid., i.

[159]Ibid., 63-70.

[160]Ibid., 63-65.

[161]Ibid., 66.

[162]Ibid., 68, 69.

[163]Ibid., 68-70. "There is no doubt that in the original text only the visitation of God was expected, since the term ἐπισκέπτομαι is used only in relationship to God."

[164]Ibid., 180-83.

[165]Émile Turdeanu, "Les Testaments des douze patriarches en slave," *JSJ* 1 (1970) 148-84.

[166]Ibid., 150-57.

[167]Ibid., 153-56, 159-60; Charles also had placed the Slavonic Version with Greek MSS aef (γ).

[168]Ibid., 166-68.

[169]Ibid., 169.

[170]Ibid.

[171]Henk Jan de Jonge, "Die Textüberlieferung der Testamente der zwölf Patriarchen," *ZNW* 63 (1972) 27-44.

[172]Ibid., 27-28. Hultgård's base was much smaller.

[173]R. H. Charles (ed.), *The Apocrypha and Pseudepigrapha of the Old Testament* (Oxford: Clarendon Press, 1913) 2. 86.

[174]J. W. Hunkin, "The Testaments of the Twelve Patriarchs," *JTS* 16 (1914) 81-89.

[175]M. de Jonge, *The Testaments of the Twelve Patriarchs* (Assen: van Gorcum, 1953) 17.

[176]M. de Jonge (ed.), *Testamenta XII Patriarcharum Edited according to Cambridge University Library MS Ff I.24 fol. 203a-262b with Short Notes* (Leiden: E. J. Brill, 1964) xiii.

[177]For MS k see de Jonge, *The Testaments* (1953) 16.

[178]Christoph Burchard, "Neues zur Überlieferung der Testamente der zwölf Patriarchen," *NTS* 12 (1965-1966) 245-47.

[179]He was unaware of Hultgård's results.

[180]H. J. de Jonge, "Die Textüberlieferung," passim.

[181]Ibid.

[182]Ibid., 29.

[183]Ibid. His analysis of MSS dlm and MS e is like that of Hultgård. His estimation of the value of MS e is, however, quite different.

[184]Ibid., 44.

[185]Ibid.

[186]Ibid.

[187]Jacob Jervell, "Ein Interpolator interpretiert," *Studien zu den Testamenten der zwölf Patriarchen* (ed. Walther Eltester; Berlin: Töpelmann, 169) 30-61.

[188]While on p. 31 Jervell is not sure that the Testaments was originally Jewish, he certainly assumes it in the rest of the article.

[189]Jervell, "Ein Interpolator interpretiert," 33-35.

[190]Ibid., 35-40.

[191]Ibid., 41.

[192]Ibid., 42-43.

[193]Ibid., 52-53.

[194]Ibid., 51.

[195]Ibid., 53.

[196]Ibid., 54.

[197]Ibid., 54-56.

[198]Ibid., 49, 58.

[199]Again, this appears to be Jervell's operating assumption although, as on p. 31, he says he is not sure.

[200]These include particularly the materials concerned with the future, the Messiah, and salvation.

[201]Johannes Thomas, "Aktuelles im Zeugnis der zwölf Väter," *Studien zu den Testamenten der zwölf Patriarchen* (ed. Walther Eltester; Berlin: Töpelmann, 1969) 62-150.

[202]Ibid., 63-70.

[203]Ibid., 71. This thesis was proposed by Meyer in 1921. See p. 37 of this study.

[204]Ibid., 73.

[205]Ibid., 73-77.

[206]Ibid., 78-79.

[207]Ibid., 80.

[208]Ibid., 80-83.

[209]Ibid., 83.

[210]Ibid.

[211]Ibid., 84-86. See also pp. 39-40 of the present study.

[212]Ibid., 88.

[213]Ibid., 92.

[214]Ibid. Thomas finds the love-of-God theme particularly in the first narration (T Jos 3:1—10:4) and the neighbor-love theme in the second (T Jos 10:5—18:4). He says that universalism already existed in the pre-Maccabean period as witnessed by Deutero-Isaiah, Jonah, and Tobit; it arose in conjunction with Israel's eschatological hope. Thomas adds, however, that some of the universalism of the Testaments is due to Christian interpolation (pp. 98-103).

[215]Ibid., 106.

[216]Ibid., 107.

[217]Ibid., 109-10.

[218]Ibid., 111-14.

[219]Ibid., 114.

[220]Ibid., 116-17.

[221]Ibid., 125-26.

[222]Ibid., 130.

[223]Ibid., 131-33.

[224]Ibid., 133.

225Ibid., 133-36.

226Ibid., 137-38.

227Ibid., 138-47.

228Louis Leloir Rev. of M. Stone, *The Testament of Levi, RQ* 7 [1970] 441-49) also discussed Jervell and Thomas and was able to affirm all three. He agreed with Stone that the Armenian Version could not be easily used to remove Christian interpolations in the Testaments; he agreed with Jervell and Thomas that the document has many obvious Christian interpolations, and finally affirmed Thomas' dating of the original Testaments.

229Peter Wallace Macky, *The Importance of the Teaching on God, Evil and Eschatology for the Dating of the Testaments of the Twelve Patriarchs,* Th.D. dissertation, Princeton Theological Seminary, 1969 (Ann Arbor, Mich.: University Microfilms, 1971).

230Ibid., 17-29.

231Ibid., 34-36.

232Ibid., 16.

233Ibid., 104-74.

234Ibid., 104-35.

235Ibid., 136-71.

236Ibid., 137-41.

237Ibid., 141-43.

238Ibid., 152-54.

239Ibid., 160-61.

240Ibid., 168.

241Ibid., 173.

242Ibid., 474-75.

243[R. H.] Charles, "The Testaments of the XII Patriarchs," *Hibbert Journal* 3 (1904-1905) 564.

244Jürgen Becker, *Untersuchungen zur Entstehungsgeschichte der Testamente der zwölf Patriarchen* (Leiden: E. J. Brill, 1970).

245Ibid., 155-56.

246Ibid., 28-43.

247Ibid., 44-68.

248Thid., 103-104

249Ibid., 105-14. Detlev Haupt ("Das Testament des Levi: Untersuchungen zu seiner Entstehung und Überlieferungsgeschichte" [Th.D. dissertation, Halle-Wittenberg, 1969] 4-5) said Becker's analysis of Gaster's Hebrew T Naphtali was correct and that Milik's supposed fragment of a Qumran T Naphtali offered such common material (Bilhah genealogy) as to be no evidence for a T Naphtali at Qumran. Haupt disagreed with Becker, however, concerning the relationship of the Aramaic T Levi materials and the T Levi of the Testaments. According to him 1) Aramaic T Levi had wide use since parts of it have been found in Cairo, at Qumran, in Greek at Mt. Athos, and in Syriac (pp. 4,6); 2) it has close parallels to the T Levi of the Testaments (p. 6); 3) it was written before the Testaments since its use was so widespread (p. 6). On this basis Haupt then offered a literary-critical analysis of the T Levi of the Testaments using in the few places possible the Aramaic T Levi parallels. His conclusions: 1) T Levi is based upon a document very near the Aramaic T Levi; 2) its purpose was to make legitimate the military-political role of the priest John Hyrcanus; 3) the present T Levi has Jewish and Christian interpolations (pp. 122-24). (Haupt's study was provided for my use by the Universitäts- und Landesbibliothek, Halle, DDR.)

250Becker, *Entstehungsgeschichte der Testamente der zwölf Patriarchen* 129-58.

251Ibid., 145.

252Ibid., 149-51.

253Ibid., 155.

254Ibid., 155-56.

255Ibid., 169-72.

256Ibid., 172-78.

[257]Ibid., 178-82.
[258]Ibid., 182-202.
[259]Ibid., 183.
[260]Ibid., 184-85.
[261]Ibid., 185-86.
[262]Ibid., 186.
[263]Ibid., 187.
[264]Ibid., 188.
[265]Ibid.
[266]Ibid., 188-90.
[267]Ibid., 188.
[268]Ibid., 189.
[269]Ibid., 189-90.
[270]Ibid., 191-95.
[271]Ibid., 191.
[272]Ibid., 192.
[273]Ibid.
[274]Ibid., 193-94.
[275]Ibid., 195.
[276]Ibid.
[277]Ibid., 197.
[278]Ibid., 198.
[279]Ibid., 199.
[280]Ibid.
[281]Ibid., 200-01.
[282]Ibid., 200.
[283]Ibid., 201.
[284]Ibid., 202.
[285]Ibid., 373.
[286]Ibid., 374.
[287]Ibid., 375-76. He places the Christian interpolations in the second century because of their use of the New Testament.

CHAPTER VII

Presuppositions, Methods, and a New Approach to the Origins Problem

The Testaments of the Twelve Patriarchs: Is it a Christian document reflecting the life and thought either of a Gentile- (de Jonge) or Jewish-Christian community (Daniélou, Milik)? Is only its final redaction Jewish-Christian (Jervell)? Or is it a Jewish document, touched but slightly by Christians, representing the Judaism of Qumran (Dupont-Sommer, Philonenko, Liver), of the Greek Diaspora (Braun, Becker), or of the Palestinian Pharisees (Charles, et al.)?

At the end of the second chapter, after having described the development of the 1884 consensus that the Testaments was a Nazarene Jewish-Christian document, we asked the question of the likely direction of future scholarship, and indicated that this might well have been to use the Testaments as a primary source for the understanding of early Jewish Christianity. With the new consensus of 1908 that the Testaments was a Jewish document, scholarship saw that its next logical steps were to let this ancient writing provide a firsthand account of the life and thought of some Jewish community. In the present state of research, however, there is no consensus concerning the origins of the Testaments, and it is most difficult in these circumstances to discuss the future direction of research in terms of the light which the Testaments sheds upon this or that ancient community.

Thus, in comparison to the situation of scholarship in 1884 and 1908, the present situation evidences an apparent setback. It might in fact be said that at no time in the history of Testaments research has less certainty prevailed than now concerning the basic issue of origins. Nonetheless, until this problem is resolved, the great worth of the Testaments as a primary source remains only potential.

If, however, the immediate question which faces scholarship is not what the Testaments reveals about one community or another, neither is it in the first place the question of origins. In the present situation it seems to me that there is a question prior to both of these, a question raised so far (if at all) only by bits and pieces, yet one that is fundamental if we are to try to move beyond the impasse over origins, namely: *What are the presuppositions and methods which have so far guided Testaments research, and why have they moved us away from rather than closer to a consensus concerning the origins of this document?*

It is this question with which the first parts of the present chapter attempt to deal. Discussion of presuppositions and methods has been rare, as the history of research shows. Nonetheless, this approach is important for the study of the Testaments, for the best use of critical methods can produce results no sounder than the presuppositions behind them. Moreover, we must consider the possibility that the critical methods themselves have been called upon to fulfill tasks beyond their capabilities. Again, the actual results of scholarship can be no better than the methods by which they were achieved. Such examples make quite clear the import of the issue of presuppositions and methods, and justify the pursuit of this question in the following pages.

Our concern with the question of presuppositions and methods is not, however, an end in itself, but serves to bring us back to the key question of Testaments origins. In the final part of the present chapter, therefore, a new approach to this question is proposed. Consistent with our analysis of presuppositions and methods and supported by the basic data of Testaments research, this new approach offers a means by which to move beyond the origins impasse.

The Presuppositions

The history of research shows that work on the origins of the Testaments had its watershed in 1884 when F. Schnapp's literary-critical study overturned nearly two hundred years of unanimous opinion concerning the origin of the document. The unstated presuppositions of scholarship regarding this question become particularly clear, therefore, as we look both backward and forward from the year 1884.

First, then, we have seen that in the period between 1700 and 1884 the Christian authorship of the Testaments was universally accepted, and for two reasons: the text of the Testaments contained clearly Christian materials, and the materials not specifically Christian were not specifically non-Christian either.[1] Thus, from 1700 to 1884 one undertook to make sense of the writing just as it stood in the MSS.[2] Becker was wrong in saying that scholarship in this period was uncritical and unable to use literary-critical tools on the text. The prominence of such tools is clear particularly in the 1850's when Kayser used them with no little subtlety to show christological differences within the Testaments. Moreover, Grabe had already raised the literary-critical question in 1698 when he suggested that the Christian materials in the document were interpolations in an originally Jewish writing. Therefore, although scholarship prior to 1884 did not follow the lead of Grabe, it was both aware of his literary-critical observation and able to use with subtlety the literary-critical method. What presuppositions kept scholarship from using this method to separate Christian and Jewish materials in the Testaments? There was but one presupposition: the Testaments with its Christian and Jewish matter could be made sense of in its totality as a Christian document.

Second, on the other side of the watershed is the period begun by Schnapp in 1884, in which the view became dominant that the Testaments is a Jewish writing containing Christian interpolations. What presuppositions stand behind this view? There is again but one: namely, it is primarily Jewish traditions which make up the content of the Testaments.[3] Interspersed are only larger or smaller amounts of Christian materials.

Thus, to scholarship before 1884 the Testaments was most easily interpreted on the basis of its Christian content. That is, the Christian content was allowed to give a Christian coloring to those materials in the document otherwise not obviously Christian. However, for Schnapp and those who followed him, it was just these same Christian materials which disrupted the integrity of an original Jewish document.

It is clear, then, that the primary data on both sides of the watershed is the same. Both before and after 1884, scholarship has consistently recognized that the Testaments contains Jewish as well as Christian materials. Indeed, already in his early evaluation of Schnapp's study, Schürer[4] argued that Christian influence on the Jewish Testaments had been far more extensive than indicated by Schnapp; and the history of research makes clear that Schürer's position has been defended repeatedly by scholars of both opposing opinions on the origins question. Only once, in fact, has the existence of Christian content in the Testaments been denied. Philonenko[5] did this in his attempt to show that the primarily messianic passages in the document refer not to the Christian Lord but, rather, to the Teacher of Qumran. Beside the fact, however, that these passages have brought to mind the Christian Messiah, the work on these passages by Chevallier[6] and Hultgård[7] makes Philonenko's interpretation of them most problematic. Moreover, the latter's picture of the Teacher of Qumran as the crucified and risen Lord of that community is, to say the least, questionable; and his narrowing of supposed Christian content to the messianic passages is, as de Jonge has pointed out, improper. For these reasons scholars have not accepted Philonenko's theory.

Since the existence of Jewish and Christian materials within the Testaments is recognized equally by scholars supporting either Jewish or Christian origins, the disagreement arises from the presuppositions by which this data is interpreted: on the one hand, it is asserted that the juxtaposition of these materials is best understood in a Christian document; on the other hand, that the removal of the Christian materials produces a coherent Jewish document.

The key question is, then: *How adequate are the presuppositions by which the data has been interpreted?* First, it must be said that these opposing presuppositions are obviously adequate in the sense that they both arise logically out of the data itself. That is, the presence of Christian materials within the Testaments leads to the possibility of Christian authorship, while the presence of Jewish tradition not clearly colored by Christian handling leads to the other possibility. Second, however, the difficulty raised by such contradictory presuppositions is that they imply two mutually exclusive views of Testaments origins, while both find support in the same data. Already at this point, therefore, we may begin to suspect a correlation between the above difficulty and the present origins dilemma.

Third, before a final decision concerning the adequacy of these presuppositions can be made, we must deal with the important issue of critical methods. Various methods have been applied to the Testaments on the basis of one presupposition or the other, in order to argue for either Jewish or Christian origins. Consequently, the results have been used as the necessary evidence in support of one presupposition or the other. In the discussion which follows, therefore, two issues become uppermost. First, How adequate are these methods for their task? Second, To what extent do they support the either/or origins presuppositions?

The Critical Methods

In developing evidence in support of one or the other of these presuppositions various critical tools are applied to the data. Therefore, in discussing the tools which have been applied by proponents of both origins theories, we shall have one primary question in mind, i.e., How suitable is each of these methods for the task assigned it by scholarship in resolving the origins dilemma?

Before beginning, however, three observations are in order. First, it should be kept in mind that the development of each of these critical methods vis-à-vis the question of Jewish or Christian origins came about initially in support of the theory of the Jewish origin of the Testaments. The history shows that this is the case, and the reasons why it is the case: proponents of Christian origins have not been compelled to find methods for excising portions of the Testaments. Jewish origins, however, can be maintained (again, as the history of research shows) only if one or another critical method illustrates convincingly that the Christian materials are secondary additions.

Second, the discussion which follows is intended to deal with the question of proper methodology rather than with actual results. The latter shall be brought into the discussion only insofar as they illustrate either problems of method, or the extent to which certain clear results make possible or obviate the use of some particular method.

Third, the history of research reveals the following chronological order in the application of critical methods to the Testaments in relationship to the origins question: literary criticism (Grabe-Kayser), text criticism (Conybeare), source criticism (Gaster), form criticism (Aschermann), motif criticism (Macky). In the present discussion, however, we shall proceed in the methodologically more proper order, beginning with text criticism and concluding with literary criticism. This order is to be preferred because source-, form-, motif-, and literary-critical results can be no sounder than the text on which they are based, while literary criticism functions properly only insofar as it takes account of source-, form-, and motif-critical results in its attempt to discover the unity of, or divergencies within, a particular document.

The Text-Critical Method

To what extent, if at all, is text criticism capable of resolving the question of the origins of the Testaments? A priori, text criticism may or may not be able to fulfill this task. That is, if it could be shown that the best MSS were free of Christian content, then this critical method would of itself resolve the origins question. On the other hand, if the best MSS include the Christian materials, then this method gives an ambiguous answer to the origins question, since the MSS might be either originally Christian or interpolated with Christian additions prior to the existence of the best MSS.

Therefore, to determine the capability of text criticism to resolve the origins question, we must move beyond a priori considerations to the actual results of scholarship in this area. As our history shows, the explicit use of text criticism in relationship to Testaments origins appeared in the attempt to provide additional support for Schnapp's theory that the Testaments was a Jewish document with later Christian additions. Conybeare and Preuschen made the claim that the shorter Armenian MSS, with their limited Christian content, were preferable to the longer MSS; and Bousset argued that the shorter Greek MSS were likewise preferable to the longer Greek MSS (especially to Cambridge University Library MS Ff I.24).

Had Conybeare, Preuschen, and Bousset been correct that the best textual witnesses did reveal the earliest accessible form of the Testaments to be without Christian content, then of course these three scholars would have resolved the origins question by the use of text criticism. This helps explain why, after the work of these scholars, research proceeded with such certainty to examine the Testaments as a Jewish document.

The history of research makes clear, however, that recent text-critical studies do not bear out the opinion of Conybeare, Preuschen, and Bousset. Taking up criticisms expressed during the First World War by Hunkin and Messel, modern textual analyses by scholars on both sides[8] of the origins dispute have shown that the earliest accessible form of the Testaments is the long text (like Cambridge University Library MS Ff I.24) used before Conybeare and containing just those Christian materials which he, Preuschen, and Bousset had hoped to eliminate on textual grounds.

Text criticism provides no evidence, therefore, for the Jewish origin of the Testaments; but neither does it prove that the Testaments was originally Christian. Why not? Because text criticism may not exclude the possibility that the extant MSS reflect only a late or "Christian" stage in the development of the Testaments. Thus, on the basis of available evidence, this method is unable to resolve the origins dilemma.

Before we leave our discussion of text criticism entirely, however, we must deal with the closely related issue of the absence of the Testaments from the Qumran discoveries. It is certainly significant for the origins question that this document does not appear among the Qumran finds. As indicated in the history of research, the assumption has arisen that the Testaments was found at Qumran. This is not true. What have been unearthed are fragments of Levi and Naphtali traditions, parts of which were well known at the beginning of this century. On the basis of analogy with the Testaments of the Twelve Patriarchs, these fragments have been designated as fragments of a Testament of Levi and a Testament of Naphtali. The designation of these as "testament" only adds to the confusion, however, since it implies not just that they have the form of testaments, but also that they may be readily equated with the Testaments of Levi and Naphtali in the Testaments. Because, however, these fragments do not have the same content as T Levi or T Naphtali, and because the loose ascription to them of the title "testament" begs an important question, we would do well to use the more neutral term "tradition," i.e., Levi traditions, Naphtali traditions. In any case, and regardless of terminology, the point remains that neither the Testaments as a whole nor any testament within the Testaments has been found among the Dead Sea materials.

This is both surprising and important. No one disagreed with Dupont-Sommer's[9] opinion that the Testaments, like its sister Jubilees, would soon appear at Qumran. What significance is there in the fact that it has not? According to Milik this means that the Testaments is probably a Christian writing; or, much less likely, it is a product of the Jewish Diaspora.[10] There are, however, other possibilities. Although a Palestinian Jewish document, the Testaments could have been written after the Dead Sea community ceased to exist, or it may simply have been unknown to that community, or unacceptable to it. Moreover, absence from Qumran would be decisive if we had the total library of the community; in fact, however, we do not.

Contrary to Milik, therefore, the absence of the Testaments from Qumran does not prove its Christian origin. More important and quite contrary to the expectations of scholarship, however, the Dead Sea discoveries have not provided us, until now at least, with MS evidence proving the Jewish origin of the Testaments. Therefore, text criticism is unable, on the basis of available evidence, to resolve the dilemma of Testaments origins.

The Source-Critical Method

On the basis of Schnapp's literary-critical conclusion that the Testaments was of Jewish origin, both text and source criticism were brought to the defense of the Jewish origin theory. Thus, source-critical arguments have been presented by Harnack, Kohler, Lévi, Cross, Eissfeldt, and Haupt to prove the Jewish origin of the Testaments. De Jonge, on the other hand, has used some of these same arguments in support of the theory that the Testaments is a Christian compilation. It is important to ask, therefore, to what extent source criticism provides an adequate tool for dealing with the origins question.

A priori, source criticism is not a tool which may be applied legitimately to the text of the Testaments in order to determine its origin. That is, source criticism per se reveals only that separate sources were used in the composition of a document. It has no way of knowing, however, *who* used them. Thus, the existence of Jewish sources within the Testaments shows only that the Testaments contains Jewish sources. It does not show whether it was a Jew or a Christian who incorporated them into the present text.

What if these sources show no signs whatsoever of Christian reworking? Source-critically this is irrelevant. Reworking becomes necessary only when a writer is either not entirely in agreement with his source or when the source must be somewhat altered for purposes of composition. Thus, were a Christian writer familiar with and sympathetic to some particular Jewish source, and were this source adequate to the purposes of the writer, there would be no need for specific "Christian" reworking. That is to say, unchanged Jewish sources can appear in an entirely Christian composition.

On the other hand, what if these sources do show signs of Christian reworking as de Jonge in the case of the Testaments has argued? This of course does not mean that the compilation in which they appear is an originally Christian document. It means only that at the compilation, redaction, or interpolation stage a Christian hand has been at work.

Concerning source criticism, therefore, we need not move beyond a priori discussion in order to show that this method is unsuited to the task sometimes assigned to it of resolving the question of the origins of the Testaments. Insofar, however, as source critical results are used by literary criticism in its analysis of the possible stages of composition of a document, then, source criticism is indeed a secondary tool in the origins search.

The Form-Critical Method

Unlike text and source criticism, only recently and in a very limited fashion has form criticism been used either in relationship to the Testaments in general or to the question of the origins of the Testaments. The strictly form-critical studies include the work of Aschermann (1954), Baltzer (2nd ed., 1964), Steck (1967), Thomas (1967), and Michel (1973). While all of them proceed upon the presupposition of the Jewish origin of the Testaments, only three (Aschermann, Baltzer, and Thomas) deal at length with the Testaments, and Aschermann alone attempts to supply further proof of Jewish origins on form-critical grounds.

The question before us again, therefore, is the propriety of using this critical method as a means of resolving the origins dilemma. The answer to this question appears clear: form criticism is no more suitable than source criticism as a *direct* means of determining the origin of the Testaments, and for similar reasons. That is, an oral or literary form is like a source in that once it exists, it stands at the service of whoever may wish to use it. There are of course two conditions placed upon this usage. First, whoever wishes to appropriate a given form (or source) must be aware that it exists; second, he must find the form suitable to his purposes.

Thus, even if the forms found in the Testaments could be documented only in Jewish sources, this would not prove that the Testaments itself was a Jewish document. That is to say, first, early Christians certainly had access to the oral and literary forms of the Jews. There is no reason therefore why a Christian familiar with a particular Jewish form might not incorporate it consciously or subconsciously in his own composition. Second, were we *not* to take this possibility most seriously, and were we to assume that all the oral and literary forms of early Christianity had the same form and stamp as those which we presently possess, then on the basis of this assumption we would obviate the need for new sources to help us uncover the mysteries of early Christian life and thought. That is, if we assume that all early Christian literature must look like that which we already possess, we take for granted that early divergence and variation does not exceed whatever is already witnessed in the present sources. More important, however, by saying that something cannot be Christian because it is not sufficiently similar to what we already know of the life and thought of the early Church, we make it actually impossible to learn anything beyond what is already known.

As a matter of fact, however, none of the form-critical studies of the Testaments has argued that the forms found within the Testaments are absent from early Christian literature. And this should be no surprise, since many of the forms used by Judaism and Christianity alike arise primarily from the Old Testament.

This does not mean that form criticism is totally irrelevant in terms of the origins question. Like source criticism, the results of form-critical studies are important to literary criticism in its attempt to determine origins and composition.

The Motif-Critical Method

Motif criticism, for lack of better terminology, is the analysis of theological themes within a document in order to determine the origin of that document. To some extent, of course, the presupposition of Jewish or Christian origins for the Testaments is a motif-critical presupposition. Thus, for example, Grabe recognized the possibility of either Jewish or Christian origins on the basis of the Jewish and Christian motifs within the Testaments; and he concluded in favor of Jewish origins because he felt that the theme of the war-like Messiah could not be the work of a Christian. As a full-blown methodology, however, motif criticism has been carried out extensively only in the recent dissertation of Macky.[11] He concludes that the Testaments must be an originally Jewish document because the themes found in it have the most parallels in the literature of current Judaism, including Qumran.

The question is, therefore, to what extent this method is capable of helping us to determine the origins of the Testaments. Our considerations begin once again with an a priori consideration. First, motif criticism is like source and form criticism in that it must recognize that once a source, form, or theological motif comes into existence, it stands at the use of anyone wishing to appropriate it. Second, it is always to be kept in mind that just as early Christianity used Jewish sources and forms, especially those found already in or developed on the basis of the Old Testament, so too it shares a wide variety of theological motifs with Judaism. Third, however, unlike source and form criticism, which are properly limited to the task of discovering sources and forms without bearing directly on the question of who used these, motif criticism has the obvious advantage that it deals with the theme *content* of these sources and forms.

How, then, is motif criticism properly used in the determination of the origins of the Testaments? It may be used only in those cases where a theological motif can arise *only* within Judaism *or* within Christianity. Thus, for example, the affirmation of Jesus' Lord- or Messiahship is a motif which distinguishes in the most essential way between Judaism and Christianity. The presence of this motif, therefore, is ipso facto proof of Christian involvement in the origins process.

Three important qualifications limit, however, the free use of motif criticism. First, if it once was possible to speak in a facile way of the "essence" of Judaism or Christianity, it clearly is not possible to do so now. The example given above is in fact one of the few motifs which does distinguish Judaism from early Christianity, because both of these phenomena are complicated and variegated. Second, it must therefore be kept in mind that motifs in the Testaments found otherwise only in (other) Jewish literature, would not serve as proof that the Testaments itself is Jewish in origin. That is, as indicated previously, once a source, form, or motif has been developed, it may be used by anyone (Jewish or Christian) who is familiar with and chooses to use it. Motifs become a basis of distinction only where we may be certain that all of the forms of early Christianity can or cannot display a particular motif. Hence, third, as was indicated in our discussion of the proper limits of form criticism, were we to limit "Christian" to what we already know from the New Testament and Church Fathers to be Christian, then we would be short-circuiting the purpose of the origins quest. That is, the primary value of the Testaments or any other similar writing as a Christian document is its potential for revealing dimensions of early Christianity not otherwise known.

None of these three qualifications to the use of motif criticism is meant to imply, however, that there are no distinctions to be drawn between Judaism and Christianity on the basis of theological motifs. To summarize our a priori discussion of this method, then, there are motifs which Judaism and Christianity do not share and which may be used to determine the Jewish or Christian origin of a document or parts of it. In general, nonetheless, we know that these two communities have the vast number of motifs in common, whether it be in the names used for God, or in the structure of the world, or in the make-up of the heavens. Moreover, the letters of Paul show us that such typically "Jewish" motifs as circumcision and sabbath found a place in some early Christian communities. Therefore, while motif criticism may properly play a direct role in the origins question, it is to be used only with the greatest care and only at those places where a particular motif simply cannot have been used by a Jewish or Christian community.

Now, looking specifically at the Testaments, what does it mean if a clearly Christian motif is found within it? This does not mean that the Testaments is Christian in origin. For example, the Christian christological affirmations in this document mean only that a Christian has been at work during some (but not necessarily the original) stage of the compilation.

What if a Jewish motif untenable within any known form of early Christianity is found in the Testaments? Here the case is somewhat different. First, it must be conceded that if a Christian used Jewish sources in the compilation of his document, occasional motifs might be found which are not entirely in accord with what we would expect from a Christian hand. But, second, clear and recurring motifs, unacceptable even within the wide variety of early Christian faith and practice, would be good evidence for the Jewish origin of the Testaments.

Our a priori discussion of the motif-critical method brings us to the conclusion, then, that it may be brought to bear directly upon the origins question but only at the point of distinctive motifs within Judaism and Christianity. The successful use of this method depends upon the nature of the contents of the Testaments.

Thus, to conclude our discussion of the ability or inability of motif criticism to resolve the origins question, we must examine Macky's extensive motif-critical study of the Testaments to see if his use of motif criticism has in fact resolved the origins question. We begin by saying once again that Macky's study is valuable in bringing together the theological themes within the Testaments and the parallels to them in the literature of Judaism and the New Testament. Nonetheless, his study suffers from serious drawbacks in its use of motif criticism to show that the Testaments is a Jewish document.

First, at the most basic level, Macky nowhere sets limits to the use of motif criticism as a tool for resolving the origins question. That is, he never raises the issue of what is distinctive to Judaism or Christianity. Rather, he operates on the assumption that the teachings in the Testaments are either Jewish or Christian depending (evidently) upon whether they are more often paralleled in Jewish or Christian literature. Thus, from the beginning Macky's use of motif criticism lacks the clarity which it should have if it is to produce convincing results vis-à-vis the origins question.

Second, then, Macky fails to acknowledge that most Christian theological motifs derive from Jewish motifs, and that both are heavily dependent upon the Old Testament and the literature and traditions related to it. This is all the more so, since the first Christians were themselves Jews.

Third, and specifically, Macky is therefore in error when, after tracing the majority of Testaments themes both in Judaism and Christianity, he concludes that these are evidence for the first century B.C.E. origin of the Testaments. Such a conclusion simply does not follow either in terms of his own data or of the proper use of motif criticism. Likewise, fourth, in those places where Macky finds parallels to Testaments motifs only within Christianity, he dismisses them when he draws his conclusions concerning origins. But in those places where he finds parallels only within Judaism, he uses these as conclusive evidence of Jewish origins.[12]

As an example of this last point, having found parallels to the angelology of the Testaments in the Jewish literature of the first century B.C.E., Macky concludes that the Testaments was written in the same period.[13] This is not, however, a proper use of motif criticism. That is, this usage establishes at best only a terminus post quem, but certainly no terminus ad quem for the appearance of any theme in angelology. Again, Macky goes beyond the proper limits of his method when he argues that the Testaments is Jewish in origin because its punishing angels motif is paralleled in Jewish but not in early Christian literature. His argumentation at this point is inadequate for various reasons. First, as we have indicated previously, motif criticism yields firm results in the question of origins only where it is able to isolate motifs clearly distinctive of Judaism or Christianity. Otherwise, second, our investigations into the life and thought of early Christianity are fatally crippled to begin with, if we assume that Christianity used no motifs beyond those attested in extant or recognized sources. Third, therefore, the use of the motif of punishing angels in Jewish literature of the first century B.C.E. does not preclude the borrowing of it later (though elsewhere unattested) by a Christian.

Thus, the results of Macky's study are inconclusive in that they are based upon an uncontrolled use of motif criticism. And while this of course does not establish that motif criticism is unable to resolve the question of Testaments origins, there are a number of indications that a resolution through this method is not probable.

One such indication is the fact that the close relationship between Judaism and Christian origins leaves little in the way of Jewish motifs which *could not* have been borrowed by some early Christian community. Another is that scholarship has claimed little in the Testaments to be distinctively Jewish, while various motifs have been claimed as distinctive of early Christian teaching or reminiscent of the New Testament. To give some idea of the actual extent to which this is so, therefore, we may draw here upon the pertinent evidence of the history of research.

T. W. Manson,[14] for example, saw in T Levi 8:4-10 a form of early Christian initiation similar to that of the Syriac Church. Vawter[15] in his "Levitical Messianism and the New Testament" argued that levitical messianism may be found nowhere in Jewish literature (including Qumran), but makes its first appearance within Christianity. This is clear particularly in Hippolytus, who bases it on Luke 1:5, 36, and in T Judah 24:1-3 and T Levi 18:6-12. Regardless of the accuracy of Vawter's view that Qumran had no levitical Messiah, his work is important in showing that this motif appeared within early Christianity. Again, L. Mariès[16] argued that the levitical messianism of the Testaments was the Jewish source for this motif within Christianity, i.e., in Hippolytus, Ambrose, and Epiphanius. Long before, Louis Ginzberg[17] had made the claim that the levitical messianism of the Testaments was a Christian interpolation based on the Epistle to the Hebrews.

Again, Roger Le Déaut,[18] in his analysis of Melchizedek as *Summus Sacerdos*, suggested that T Levi 3:5-6 and the earliest Roman canon are similar in their discussion of the priest's offering of a "reasonable and bloodless sacrifice." And Joachim Gnilka[19] in his "Der Hymnus des Zacharias" studied Luke's Benedictus with its messianic $\dot{\alpha}\nu\alpha\tau o\lambda\grave{\eta}$ $\dot{\epsilon}\xi$ $\ddot{v}\psi o v s$ and found its only close parallel in T Judah 24:1-6.

Perhaps of more value than the above, however, is the work of Macky.[20] Since it is his primary conclusion that the Testaments was written at the same time as the Qumran literature,[21] we must take seriously those places in the Testaments where he found the best parallels to this document not in Qumran, but in Christianity. The number of such places is not insignificant, as Macky himself said in his introduction.[22] The following provides some indication of such Christian-Testaments motifs, and is drawn from Macky's discussion of the picture of God in the Testaments.[23]

Concerning titles of God, for example, Macky pointed out that Holy Father[24] and God of Peace[25] appear only in the Testaments and in the New Testament. The other titles are common to the whole period of "late" Judaism and the Old Testament.[26] Concerning God's transcendence Macky indicated that the use of the seven heavens in T Levi is an interpolation, because it appears only within Christianity and post-Christian Judaism.[27] Concerning accessible transcendence he said that T Levi and Revelation are very close, and that this closeness is based on the use of Enoch traditions by both. In terms of God's indwelling, Macky concluded that only the Testaments and First John are similar.[28] We see here, then, that by Macky's own admission the Testaments offers significant elements uniquely shared with early Christianity.

Similarly, the older studies of themes, done by scholars who defended the Jewish origin of the Testaments, show the presence of Christian motifs within the Testaments. Foremost among these is that of God-neighbor love and forgiveness. According to Charles,[29] such a teaching is found only in the Testaments and New Testament, and nowhere else in ancient Judaism. Similarly, Lagrange argued that the universalism of the Testaments has parallels in this period only within Christianity.[30] And Herford[31] saw the universalism and God-neighbor love material uniquely close to the teaching of Jesus.

When we move on to reminiscences of the New Testament in the Testaments, the situation is the same. Over the whole course of research the issue of possible parallels and dependencies between the Testaments and New

Testament has been raised. Vorstman[32] is the first to show parallels between various New Testament writings and the Testaments, although he argued that 1 Thess 2:16 alone was actually quoted (T Levi 6:11) by the author of the Testaments. Preceding Vorstman, Dorner[33] compiled from various sections of the Testaments a complete description of Jesus' person and work similar to that in the Gospels. Moreover, not long after Vorstman, Warfield[34] argued that the writer of the Testaments was familiar with nearly every writing in the New Testament canon. While Warfield's work was self-admittedly an apology against the Tübingen School, Sinker[35] also presented a lengthy list of Testaments-New Testament similarities like Vorstman's.

Discussion of parallels between the New Testament and Testaments did not end, however, with the beginning of the new period in 1884. Harnack[36] was convinced of the Jewish origin of the Testaments, but used Warfield's article as proof of the extensive Christian interpolation of the document. On the other hand, Charles[37] offered a large number of parallels particularly between Matthew and the Testaments in order to indicate how deeply the Testaments had influenced the New Testament and Jesus himself. Similarly, according to A. W. Argyle four significant elements of the Gospel picture of Jesus were shaped by the portrayal of Joseph in the Testaments.[38] To Plummer,[39] however, Charles' extensive parallels between the Testaments and Jesus' teaching in Matthew indicated not that Jesus had used the Testaments (otherwise the parallels would be equally scattered in the Synoptic Gospels), but that a Christian interpolator familiar especially with Matthew had added these Jesus traditions to the Testaments.

But if Matthew and the Testaments seem to have special affinities, so do the Johannine writings and the Testaments, according to Stauffer and Cyril Richardson. Stauffer[40] offered a long list of parallels between the Testaments and John/First John, while Richardson[41] has argued for the dependence of the Testaments upon certain verses in First John.

Thus, while motif criticism may be the proper tool in some cases for determining the origin of a particular document, it is much less useful for the Testaments because of the nature of the contents of this writing. That is, there is little in the "Jewish" content of the Testaments of which a Christian might not also have availed himself. If, on the other hand, there do appear to be motifs distinctive of Christianity within the Testaments, this does not prove the Christian origin of the document. As indicated earlier, it shows only that a Christian hand was involved at some stage in the composition. To conclude, then, the nature of the content of the Testaments makes the successful application of motif criticism to the origins question extremely difficult.

The Literary-Critical Method

Having discussed the limits of the use of text, source, form, and motif criticism in relationship to the question of the origins of the Testaments, we come now to literary criticism. Unlike our discussion of the other methods, however, there is no need to determine the legitimacy of this method to deal with the question of Testaments origins. This is because the literary-critical method has the inherent task of dealing with just such questions.

Conceding a positive answer to the theoretical question, we are brought therefore to the specific issue of literary criticism's ability to achieve successful results given the nature of the Testaments and the origins problem posed by it. Thus, already in 1891 W. J. Deane[42] criticized Schnapp's literary-critical analysis of the Testaments on four grounds. First, he said that such a method would not work successfully on the Testaments, because this document lacked the clear sutures needed to show stages of interpolation. Second, it would not work because the style and language of the Testaments was consistent throughout; third, it lacked external textual verification. Fourth, in the light of these three facts, literary criticism would simply prove its own presuppositions.

Particularly at the present point in Testaments research, it is important to take Deane's criticisms seriously. First, it remains true that literary criticism is always in danger of proving its own presuppositions. This is especially so in the case of the Testaments. The basic data of "Jewish" and Christian content lends itself too easily to the obvious conclusion that an original Jewish document comes to light as soon as the Christian materials in the Testaments are labelled as interpolated, and removed.

Second, this danger is increased all the more when, as Deane says, there are few external controls for literary-critical conclusions. Such, however, is the present situation. That is, our discussion of text criticism indicated that in the present state of scholarship it is very difficult to remove Christian materials from the Testaments on textual grounds. Thus, for example, neither Becker nor Hultgård is able to depend heavily upon text-critical support for his literary-critical omission of Christian elements from the Testaments.

Third, although Deane is wrong in his assertion that the Testaments lacks sutures, it must be kept in mind that these may be marks of compilation rather than signs of interpolation. Source-critical studies of the Testaments support this possibility. In such a case, therefore, sutures might be produced *either* by the original compiler bringing together divergent sources and his own contributions, or by an interpolator or redactor.

Fourth, and ancillary to the above, while it is not to be denied that sutures appear within the Testaments, the extent of these has been magnified disproportionately for students who have come to know the Testaments through the English and Greek text published by R. H. Charles. His combination of the readings of short and long texts, and his parentheses and brackets give the impression that the Testaments is one non sequitur upon another. Quite another impression is given the reader, however, who follows the text as it actually exists, i.e., for example in MS Ff I.24, rather than in the artificial form in which Charles presents it.[43]

Fifth, while form criticism was unknown to Deane, it now plays an important part in support of his position. Specifically, Schnapp had argued that the apocalyptic or future sections of each testament had no relationship to the historical and paraenetic sections. According to him, therefore, these future sections were interpolations. Modern form criticism has shown, however, that whether the Testaments is classified formally in conjunction with the farewell discourse, covenant formula, or prophetic judgment word, it properly concludes its historical and paraenetical sections with prophetic materials. This means, then, that the Christian materials prominent in these future sections cannot be excluded from the Testaments simply because they appear within an apocalyptical context.

We started with W. J. Deane's conclusion that literary criticism plays no proper role in the search for the origins of the Testaments. Nothing of the above was meant to imply, however, that Deane was correct in this opinion. On the contrary, it falls specifically within the task of this method to deal with the question of Testaments origins. This is all the more so since the actual results of textual and motif criticism leave the possibility of Jewish or Christian origins open, while source and form criticism do not have it within their capabilities to resolve this problem. That is to say, if the problem is to be resolved, the task falls to literary criticism.

Nonetheless, as previously indicated, the inability of these other critical methods to solve the dilemma makes the results of literary criticism all the more precarious by failing to provide them with the additional supports needed for a method which tends to confirm its own presuppositions. In fact, while text and motif criticism do not provide external support for literary-critical conclusions, source and form criticism have complicated the literary-critical task.

Nor may we fail to mention at this point the actual results of the application of this method to the Testaments. It has produced no consensus concerning the specific place of and evidence for the particular sutures claimed by it. Again, this is not to say that such sutures do not exist. Given the most divergent claims concerning their extent, however, it is fair to say that literary criticism has not so far produced satisfying results.

This does not mean that it will be unable to do so in the future. What it does mean is that literary-critical results vis-à-vis the Testaments must be treated with caution, particularly since modern scholarship (especially text criticism) has tended to remove the external controls so important to the successful and convincing use of literary criticism.

The Critical Methods — A Summary

The history of Testaments research showed us that five critical methods have been applied to the Testaments for the purpose of revealing the origins of this document. In considering the question of the intrinsic capability of each method to deal with the problem, we excluded at the outset source and form criticism from a direct role in the origins search, since a Jew or a Christian might make use of Old Testament and later Jewish sources and forms. In the case of text, motif, and literary criticism, however, we concluded that each of these three methods may be brought to bear directly on the problem of Testaments origins. Therefore, it was necessary to ask of each of these a second question, namely, Given the actual results of scholarship, to what extent do text, motif, and literary criticism actually bring us closer to a solution of the origins dilemma?

Text criticism has not provided decisive information for solving the dilemma because it leaves the "Jewish" and Christian materials within the Testaments intact, and it provides little evidence for separating out any original Jewish document. Yet, on the other hand, its inability to exclude the Christian materials from the Testaments does not prove the Christian origin of the document either, since these might have been added to an original Jewish writing at any time before the creation of our earliest textual witnesses.

Motif criticism may be expected to work successfully only when brought to bear on those motifs in the Testaments distinctive to either Judaism or Christianity. But, as Macky's study makes clear, most are in fact common to Judaism and its child, Christianity. Thus, given the nature of the contents of the Testaments, motif criticism appears incapable of finding the distinctive Jewish materials which would be evidence for an original Jewish Testaments. Moreover, motif criticism cannot tell us whether these materials belong to the original document or were added at a redactional or interpolative stage.

Literary criticism certainly should be able to solve the problem. Its task, however, has become harder rather than easier as the actual results of scholarship have come in. That is, text criticism no longer provides blanket permission for the excision of Christian materials from the Testaments. Source criticism warns us that what were thought to be signs of redaction or interpolation may also be signs of compilation. Motif criticism shows us that there is little in the Testaments which could not be Christian, while there is much which seems to be. And literary criticism itself has not yet produced a consensus. This does not mean we are to cease our endeavors along these lines. Even with the exercise of perfect care, however, we must keep in mind that literary criticism, *unless external controls are found for it*, will still tend to prove its own presuppositions.

Text, source, form, motif, and literary criticism: when applied to the Testaments on the basis of the presuppositions of the Jewish or Christian authorship of this document, these critical methods do not provide a sure grasp upon the slippery nut of the origins dilemma.

A More Inclusive Approach

Already in the early 1950s, as previously indicated, H. F. D. Sparks argued that the results of scholarship had left it very doubtful whether this document was valuable for our understanding of either Judaism or early Christianity. The above analysis of past presuppositions and methods would appear also to bear out Sparks' opinion. Therefore, if we are not willing to settle for such a view of things, we must find a new approach to the origins question. It is the purpose of the final section of the present chapter to do this.

Put simply, I propose that we cease dealing with the origins question on the basis of either/or presuppositions. This is not to say that such presuppositions are inherently false. My proposal is, however, that we work on the basis of what might be called both/and presuppositions. The same data is of course involved, but where an either/or treatment of it has helped to bring us to the present cul-de-sac, a more inclusive approach may produce fruitful results for both Judaism and early Christianity.

Eyebrows may be raised by the suggestion that we should begin to look at the Testaments as a document of both Jewish and Christian origin, since that does not seem to be logically possible. It may be in fact just for this reason that scholarship has clung consciously or subconsciously to its either/or presuppositions. Such logic fails to take account, however, of the fundamental purposes behind our quest for Testaments origins. We do not seek to resolve the issue of origins in an abstract sense, but to determine the community or communities portrayed in the Testaments. And, basically, we seek to enhance our knowledge of the varieties of life and thought in such communities.

At the abstract level, therefore, our either/or presuppositions apply, since the Testaments originated at some point in time within either a Jewish or a Christian community. At the level where this document illuminates the life and thought of particular communities, however, our either/or presuppositions need no longer apply. This is the case because the basic data of Testaments research, i.e., the Jewish and Christian content of the Testaments, makes possible the double origin of the document. It makes room for the possibility, that is, that this source may reveal the contours of life in both Jewish and Christian communities.

Such an inclusive approach has the additional and very important advantage also that it is justified by the critical methods which have been brought to bear on the origins question. Thus in the previous pages we have shown that text-critical studies do not support either/or presuppositions, but indicate that the text of the Testaments in its earliest known form combines Jewish and Christian materials. Similarly, we argued that neither source nor form criticism is equipped to determine the Jewish or Christian origin of the Testaments, because Jewish sources and forms (especially those in the Testaments) were available as the common property of Jews and Christians. Exactly for this reason, however, both source and form criticism support a both/and approach to the question of Testaments origins. Again, our discussion of motif or content criticism argued that the vast majority of Testaments themes could be construed as both Jewish and Christian. And, finally, in considering the literary-critical method, we concluded that it alone may have the means to separate Jewish from Christian within the Testaments. This task of literary criticism is itself evidence, however, that the Testaments should be dealt with from the perspective both of Judaism and Christianity.

The Testaments from the Perspective of Judaism

What concrete form does our proposed approach take, therefore, in dealing with the Testaments as a witness to the life and thought of some Jewish community? On the basis of our analysis of critical methods applied to the question of Testaments origins, it appears clear that any treatment of this document from the perspective of Judaism will fall back primarily, as Becker and Hultgård have recently reasserted, upon literary criticism. New discoveries like those of Qumran may some day turn up a Testaments free of Christian content, but the absence of the Testaments as a whole and of any individual testament from the Qumran finds themselves probably diminishes the chances of such a discovery elsewhere. Similarly, while yet unknown Greek and Armenian MSS may in the future reveal to us a less- or non-Christian text of the Testaments, the present tendency of research in this area is the affirmation of the textual integrity of the Christian portions of the Testaments.

The responsibility falls primarily, therefore, upon the literary-critical method if a Jewish Testaments is to be convincingly reconstructed from the extant form of this document. Whether and to what extent this method will be able to produce more conclusive results than in the past is not at issue here. Its dangers and pitfalls, especially in a case like that of the Testaments, have already been discussed. Regardless of the difficulties which beset it, however, literary criticism is the only available method for providing us with a Jewish Testaments of the Twelve Patriarchs.

The Testaments from the Perspective of Early Christianity

Such a continuing quest for a Testaments which illuminates some part of Judaism in no way hinders the analysis of this document as a witness to some form of early Christianity. Such an analysis is justified by the results both of text and motif criticism, by our consideration of the basic neutrality of source and form criticism in documents like the Testaments, and by the necessary role of literary criticism in attempting to reconstruct a purely Jewish document from a document which at present is not purely Jewish.

Along what lines are we to proceed, then, in dealing with the Testaments from the perspective of early Christianity? To begin with, we must recall our discussion of the fact that much of the content of the Testaments is not of an obvious Christian nature, but is instead "Jewish" or, better phrased, *ambiguous* in origin. This raises a serious question: How can we treat a document composed in large part of "Jewish" or ambiguous traditions as a witness to some form of early Christianity? This question is, as previously indicated, at the very heart of Jewish origins theories, and causes serious difficulty for any attempt to look at the Testaments from a Christian perspective. In terms of our proposed both/and approach, therefore, the following discussion must deal specifically with just this question.

First, then, in our analysis of the use of source, form, and motif criticism in terms of the dilemma of Testaments origins, one particular consideration was very important. That is, given the existence of any piece of tradition with a known origin, the presence of such a tradition within a document gives no indication of the origin of that document. Its presence means only that the writer of the document must be familiar with the tradition and basically in sympathy with it. In other words, once a tradition (source, form, or motif) exists, it stands at the service of anyone who wishes to use it.

What does this consideration mean for the Testaments? It means that the existence of "Jewish" traditions within the Testaments bears little relationship to the question of the person(s) who used these in the Testaments. That is, because this person draws upon "Jewish" tradition does not mean that he is necessarily a Jew, or only a Jew. It means simply that he knows and finds these traditions useful to his own purpose.

Second, and more particularly, however, What is the significance of the fact that, as Sparks said, it is most difficult to conceive of the Testaments as a Christian document because most of the materials within it are not obviously Christian? We must discuss this question now in terms of each of the types of materials which appear within the Testaments, i.e., in terms of its traditions about the Patriarchs, in terms of its paraenesis, and of its messianic/apocalyptic sections.[44]

The first large segment of materials in each testament is made up of traditions about the Patriarchs of the Old Testament. These traditions have their origin in Old Testament stories and later haggadic extensions of them. Is this material, therefore, Jewish and not Christian? That it appears to be Jewish is the obvious conclusion, because it is derived from the Old Testament. But this obvious conclusion need not be correct. De Jonge, for example, sees in much of the Joseph tradition in the Testaments a typology between Jesus and Joseph. Regardless of the accuracy of this assertion, however, and even if no clearly Christian material appears in the traditions concerning the Fathers, it would still not be true that this material is more Jewish than Christian. Why? Because the Old Testament was the Bible of the early Church. This fact has not been taken with sufficient seriousness in past discussion. It means that these Jewish traditions are *at the same time* Christian traditions, and that the persons and events in them are, from an early Christian understanding, Christian. It is correct to say, therefore, that the large block of haggadic material which appears in the Testaments is Jewish, because the Old Testament is Jewish. However, Christianity claimed as its own many of these same traditions; and this means that their appearance in the Testaments may be due no less to Christian than to Jewish handling.

One may argue, of course, that a Christian would not use such Old Testament materials without giving them distinctive Christian coloring. We might think of Paul's use of Abraham traditions within the context of a discussion of a central point of Christian theology. On the other hand, however, and exclusive of the fact that de Jonge has indicated such Christian coloring, it is also necessary to understand the *function* of the patriarchal narratives in the Testaments before expecting Christian coloring. These narratives serve primarily as an introduction to the paraenesis of this document. That is, on the basis of the narratives, each Patriarch offers advice for the conduct of his children. In this context and function we need expect no Christian coloring, since the "Jewish" traditions themselves are sufficient to the purpose of the Testaments at this point.

To summarize, for early Christians the Old Testament is no less a Christian than a Jewish document, and traditions from it are the common property of both communities. To say that these traditions in the Testaments do not have sufficient Christian coloring is false on two grounds: they are already understood to be Christian, and in their present function require none of the obvious Christian coloring present for example in the use of Abraham by Paul. Nothing in the above should be understood to mean, however, that these traditions in the Testaments are necessarily Christian. They are simply, setting aside de Jonge's work in this discussion, ambiguous. Nonetheless, "ambiguous" is an important word, because it means that as the reader goes through the first section of each testament and does not find overt Christian coloring, he should not conclude that the material is too Jewish to be Christian.

The second large segment of materials within the Testaments is composed of ethical paraenesis introduced through the narratives of the past deeds, good and bad, of the Patriarchs. On the basis of these deeds each Patriarch advises his children how to conduct their lives. Is this material Jewish or Christian? For the most part, it may certainly be brought under the wide umbrella of Judaism. There is no need to dispute this by discussing the curious absence of reference to the ritual elements of the Law, i.e., Sabbath and circumcision, nor by discussing remarkable parallels between the ethics of the Testaments and early Christianity. But the fact that the material is Jewish does not mean that it is not Christian. Again, as with the narratives, the primary point of origin of the paraenesis is the Old Testament, the common property of Judaism and Christianity. While most of the individual ethical teachings are easily paralleled in Jewish literature, so are they also, and in some instances more easily, paralleled in early Christian literature.

Again, however, the question might be asked why this paraenesis does not show distinctive Christian coloring, but appears to be ambiguous. Three considerations are important at this point. First, a Christian author, and those for whom he is writing, would already be aware of his Christian perspective. This becomes a problem only for those, like us, who no longer know the origin of the document. Second, the paraenesis has behind it the authority of the Patriarchs of the Scriptures and needs *no other* overtly Christian authority to justify it. Third, and most important, paraenesis tends to have a characteristic ambiguity about it. In Jas 1:2-18, for example, we also have paraenetical material with no Christian coloring. In Jas 2:2-13, similar to the Testaments in its reference to the Law and neighbor-love command, we have no more Christian coloring than in the Testaments. Again, the *Haustafel* in Col

3:18—4:1 is, with the exception of the conclusion, without Christian coloring. Finally, in Gal 5:19-21 we have the following illuminating text:

> Now the work of the flesh is plain: immorality, impurity, licentiousness, idolatry, sorcery, enmity, strife, jealousy, anger, selfishness, dissension, party spirit, envy, drunkenness, carousing, and the like. I warn you, as I warned you before, that those who do such things shall not inherit the kingdom of God.[45]

This text is interesting to us for two reasons. First, the Testaments could be an exposition of it, since parts of the paraenesis of the Testaments are devoted to almost all of these "works of the flesh." Second, there is nothing in this text which is "Christian."

That these paraenetical examples from the New Testament are in their individual contexts Christian is not to be doubted. The verses immediately surrounding each paraenetical section alone make this clear. Nonetheless, from the paraenesis itself this is not obvious. What this means for the question of the origin of the Testaments is simply that the second segment of materials, the ethical paraenesis, does not tell us if the writer was a Jew or a Christian. Our examples from the New Testament show us that paraenetical materials without Christian coloring in themselves gain that coloring only within the context of the Christian setting, i.e., within James, Colossians, and Galatians. Paraenesis does not in fact need an obvious Christian content in order to be effective among its Christian hearers; its effectiveness stems directly from the authority of the one who speaks or writes it, i.e., from Paul or James, or, in the case of the Testaments, from the Patriarchs.

We come at this point, then, to the decisive phase of this part of our discussion. We have said that it is the context of the ambiguous paraenetical materials which shows their real color. The discussion of this context takes us immediately to the third segment of materials in the Testaments, the messianic/apocalyptic.

The patriarchal narratives and the ethical paraenesis derived from these narratives are ambiguous, at least as it has been argued above, in that they give no sure evidence concerning the background of the person(s) who structured them into their present form in the Testaments. It has not been denied above that these materials are Jewish. To this point, then, Sparks is correct: much of the material in the Testaments is "Jewish." It is not, however, uniquely or unambiguously so. That is, a Jewish writer addressing his community or a Christian addressing his could draw equally upon the same traditions. It is here, as it seems to me, that Sparks is incorrect: the use of these narratives and paraenesis of Jewish origin does not tell us who used them in the Testaments.

What, then, does tell us this? As indicated above, clues to the Jewish or Christian provenance of the writer come only through the overall context of the writing. Specifically, we may expect to find such clues especially at those places within the Testaments in which distinctive aspects of Judaism and Christianity are treated. These elements do not appear in the first and second segments of Testaments materials, but in the third segment, the

messianic/apocalyptic. It is, after all, at this point in the early Church that the
πέτρα σκανδάλου makes its appearance, for in the particular designation of
the Christian Lord as Messiah, Judaism and Christianity have their clear
separation.

What do we find in this third segment of Testaments materials? The
reference is to the Christian Lord. Whether only redactionally, as Grabe,
Schnapp, Bousset, Harnack, Schürer, van der Woude, Jervell, Becker, and
Hultgård have said, or whether originally, as the 18th and 19th centuries, de
Jonge and his supporters have argued, the messianic Lord of the Testaments is
one and the same as that of the New Testament. The history of research is
uniform, with the exception of Philonenko, at this point.

We have discussed the three recurrent types of material within the
Testaments, and have argued that the first two are ambiguous and may be
credited either to a Jew or a Christian. In the third type, however, where we
might expect the distinction between a Jewish and a Christian writer to be
clear, we see that the history of research does provide a uniform answer: the
messianic figure in the present form of the Testaments is the Christian Lord.
Now, however, from here we may work backward to the ambiguous segments
and see them in the context in which they presently stand, i.e., a Christian
context. We are called upon, therefore, to read the Testaments from a new
perspective. We must attempt to put aside the question, Is the Testaments
originally Jewish, or is it originally Christian? Rather, granted the present
Christian context, we need to let this provide coloring for the ambiguous
narrative and paraenetical materials. That is, we need to read backward in the
Testaments with the awareness that the narratives and ethical paraenesis have
as their *present conclusion* messianic prophecy, the focus of which is the
Christian Lord.

Conclusion

On the basis of the history of research in Chapter 2 through Chapter 6 of
the present study, we have sought in this last chapter to clarify and analyze the
presuppositions and methods which have governed scholarship in its
examination of the Testaments of the Twelve Patriarchs. We have done this
for two reasons. First, the history of research itself shows us that past
presuppositions and methods have not produced convincing results in terms
of the dilemma of Testaments origins. Second, the history reveals also that
these presuppositions and methods have received little consideration per se,
while in fact the successful results of scholarship depend in large measure
upon the propriety of just such presuppositions and methods.

The more inclusive approach advanced in the final section of this chapter
is proposed in the belief that it is commensurate both with the basic data of
Testaments research and with the critical methods by which this data is to be
interpreted. This approach does not seek to deal with the question of origins at
an abstract level, but rather at that level where the Testaments actually
witnesses to the life and thought of particular communities.

In a sense, there is little which might be called new in the final section of the present chapter. No new methods are proposed, although some old ones are qualified; and no new evidence is brought forth. What is offered, however, is a different orientation to the origins question, one which allows us to take all of the evidence seriously and, at the same time, to deal with the Testaments from the perspective both of Jewish and Christian communities. This orientation does not make the analysis of the Testaments from the Jewish perspective an easy task, because it demands of literary criticism both the accuracy and the external controls so hard to achieve in the case of the Testaments. From the Christian perspective it calls for a reading of the Testaments from *end to beginning*.

At the beginning of our study we said that the real value of the Testaments of the Twelve Patriarchs is its use as a primary source for the way of life of some ancient community or communities of faith. Concern with this issue, however, has brought me to the conviction that it cannot be handled properly without first dealing with the easily forgotten and less exciting matters of presuppositions and methods within the history of Testaments research.

In the present study these matters have been given the serious consideration long overdo them; we are now able, therefore, to take up the quest of the type of community(ies) revealed in an eyewitness fashion by the Testaments. Perhaps literary criticism or new Qumran-like discoveries or new MSS may yet illuminate convincingly a Jewish Testaments of the Twelve Patriarchs. The contents of this final chapter indicate, however, that a quest for the origins of the Testaments in some form of early Christianity is not only possible and justified, but also compelled by the nature of the document, by modern critical developments, and by the many-faceted character of Christian religion in its early forms.

In this sense, then, the present study becomes a prolegomenon to the quest for the ancient Christian community which redacted or composed the Testaments. But having come this far, the work ahead is hardly simple. If the Testaments bears witness to a Pauline or Gentile fellowship, it is difficult to explain the close proximity to or awareness of Jewish traditions. If the Testaments represents a narrow "Judaizing" of the faith, it is not easy to explain the universal outlook of the document. We are not to wonder, therefore, that proponents of Christian origins in the eighteenth and nineteenth centuries could not place the Testaments with certainty in any one of the then known early Christian communities. Although there is no direct evidence to support it, one might conjecture that scholarship's climactic reversal of 1884 from Christian to Jewish origins was produced at least in part by just this inability of scholarship to make a neat identification between the Testaments and the then known Christian communities.

Such difficulties, however, rather than causing us to throw up our arms in despair, should be major reasons for pursuing the quest with all the more interest, since they reveal that the Testaments may witness to a community of Christian faith previously unknown in existing primary and even, perhaps, secondary sources. There is of course no space to devote to such a quest in the present study, because this work has limited itself intentionally to research history, its presuppositions, and methods. But with this study, the necessary ground has been cleared and the way opened for a proper appreciation of the Testaments and especially of the Christian community in which it lived.

FOOTNOTES

[1]See Robert Sinker, *The Testaments of the XII Patriarchs* (Cambridge: Deighton, Bell and Co., 1869) 122; Johannes Marinus Vorstman, *Disquisitio de Testamentorum XII Patriarcharum* (Rotterdam: P. C. Hoog, 1857) 91-101; Joseph Langen, *Das Judenthum in Palästina zur Zeit Christi* (Freiburg: Herder'sche Verlagshandlung, 1866) 140-57.

[2]That is, as it stood in Cambridge University Library MS Ff I.24.

[3]See Johannes Ernestus Grabius (ed.), *Spicilegium SS. Patrum ut et Haereticorum, seculi post Christum natum I. II. III* (Oxford: [n.n.], 1698) 1. 139; M. Gaster, "The Hebrew Text of One of the Testaments of the Twelve Patriarchs," *Society of Biblical Archaeology: Proceedings* 16-17 (1894) 37-39; Adolf Harnack, *Geschichte der altchristlichen Litteratur bis Eusebius* (Leipzig: J. C. Hinrichs'sche Buchhandlung, 1897) 1. 566.

[4]See p. 21 of the present study.

[5]See pp. 60-61 of the present study.

[6]See pp. 54-55 of the present study.

[7]See pp. 71-72 of the present study.

[8]This becomes particularly clear in the recent studies by Hultgård and Becker. Both begin with lengthy text-critical analyses, but turn finally to literary criticism in order to remove Christian interpolations from the Testaments. Thus Hultgård says specifically (*Croyances messianiques des Test. XII Patr.* [Upsala: Skriv Service AB, 1971] 180-83) that text criticism is unable to remove most Christian messianic references from the Testaments.

[9]André Dupont-Sommer, *Nouveaux aperçus sur des manuscrits de la mer Morte* (Paris: Maisonneuve, 1953) 63.

[10]J. T. Milik, rev. of M. de Jonge, *The Testaments, RB* 62 (April 1955) 298.

[11]See pp. 78-79 of this study.

[12]See p. 79 of this study.

[13]See p. 79 of this study.

[14]See p. 39 of this study.

[15]See p. 65 of this study.

[16]L. Mariès, "Le messie issu de Lévi chez Hippolyte de Rome," *RevScRel* 39 (1959) 381-96.

[17]Louis Ginzberg, "Eine unbekannte jüdische Sekte," *Monatschrift für Geschichte und Wissenschaft des Judentums* 58 (1914) 395-409.

[18]See p. 65 of this study.

[19]See pp. 65 of this study.

[20]See pp. 78-79 of this study.

[21]Peter Wallace Macky, *The Importance of the Teaching on God, Evil and Eschatology for the Dating of the Testaments of the Twelve Patriarchs*, Th.D. dissertation, Princeton Theological Seminary, 1969 (Ann Arbor, Mich.: University Microfilms, 1971) 474-75.

[22]Ibid., 8-16.

[23]Ibid., 37-103.

[24]Ibid., 73.

[25]Ibid., 74.

[26]Ibid., 69-73.

[27]Ibid., 79.

[28]Ibid., 96-101.

[29]See p. 28-29 of this study.

[30]See p. 37 of this study.

[31]See p. 38 of this study.

[32]Vorstman, *Disquisitio de Testamentorum XII Patriarcharum* 105-47.

[33]See p. 9 of this study.

[34]B. B. Warfield, "The Apologetical Value of the Testaments of the Twelve Patriarchs," *Presbyterian Review* I (1880) 58-84.

[35]Robert Sinker, *The Testaments of the XII Patriarchs* 209.

[36]Adolf Harnack, *Geschichte der altchristlichen Litteratur bis Eusebius* 1. 570.

[37]R. H. Charles (ed.), *The Testaments of the Twelve Patriarchs, Translated from the Editor's Greek Text* (London: Adam and Charles Black, 1908) lxxv-xcii.

[38]A. W. Argyle, "The Influence of the Testaments of the Twelve Patriarchs upon the New Testament," *ExpT* 63 (1951-1952) 256-58.

[39]Alfred Plummer, "The Relations of the Testaments of the Patriarchs to the Books of the New Testament," *The Expositor*, 7th ser. 6 (1908) 489-491.

[40]Ethelbert Stauffer, *Die Theologie des Neuen Testaments* (Genf: Oikumene Verlag, 1945) 318-21.

[41]I received this information from Professor Richardson in mimeographed form.

[42]See p. 21 of this study.

[43]Although no modern English translation of this Cambridge University Library MS exists, Robert Sinker's 19th century translation is useful at this point. It is found in Alexander Roberts and James Donaldson, eds., *The Ante-Nicene Fathers: Translations of the Writings of the Fathers down to A.D. 325* (reprint ed., Grand Rapids: Wm. B. Eerdmans Publishing Company, 1951) 8. 9-38. Hunkin (p. 36 above) called Charles' approach a "scissors and paste" method for removing Christian interpolations.

[44]Such is the normal designation of these materials. Their actual content is a description of future events both in "this world" and in "the world to come." The reference to two different futures has gone unnoticed, but bears very directly, I believe, upon the role of two Messiahs and a single royal Messiah in the Testaments.

[45]The text is quoted here according to the Revised Standard Version of the Bible.

Bibliography

A. Research of the Pre-Schnapp Period

[Corrodi, Heinrich.] *Kritische Geschichte des Chiliasmus.* 2 vols. Leipzig: [n.n.], 1781.

Dillmann, A. "Pseudepigraphen des Alten Testaments." *Real-Encyclopädie für protestantische Theologie und Kirche* 12 (1883): 341-67.

Dorner, I. A. *Entwicklungsgeschichte der Lehre von der Person Christi von den ältesten Zeiten bis auf die neuesten.* 3 vols. 2nd ed. Stuttgart: Samuel Gottlieb Lisching, 1845-1856.

_____. *History of the Development of the Doctrine of the Person of Christ.* Translated by William Lindsay Alexander. 5 vols. Edinburgh: T. and T. Clark, 1861-1863.

Ewald, Heinrich. *Geschichte des Volkes Israel.* 8 vols. 3rd ed. Göttingen: Dieterichsche Buchhandlung, 1864-1868.

Fabricius, Johan. Albertus, ed. *Codex pseudepigraphus Veteris Testamenti, collectus, castigatus testimoniisque, censuris et animadversionibus illustratus.* 2 vols. 2nd ed. Hamburg: Theodori Christoph. Felginer, 1722.

Gallandi, Andrea, ed. *Bibliotheca veterum patrum antiquorumque scriptorum ecclesiasticorum postrema Lugdunensi longe locupletior etque accuratior.* 14 vols. Venice: Joannio Baptistae Albrittii Hieron., 1765-1781.

Geiger, Abraham. "Apokryphen zweiter Ordnung." *Jüdische Zeitschrift für Wissenschaft und Leben* 7 (1869): 116-35.

Grabius, Johannes Ernestus, ed. *Spicilegium SS. Patrum ut et Haereticorum, seculi post Christum natum I. II.& III.* 2 vols. Oxford: [n.n.], 1698.

Hengel, W. A. van. *De Testamenten der twaalf Patriarchen op nieuw ter Sprache gebragt.* Amsterdam: Ten Brink & de Vries, 1860.

Hilgenfeld, A. "Das Urchristentum und seine neuesten Bearbeitungen von Lechler und Ritschl." *Zeitschrift für wissenschaftliche Theologie* 1 (1858): 377-440.

_____. Review of Robert Sinker, *The Testaments of the XII Patriarchs. Zeitschrift für wissenschaftliche Theologie* 14 (1871): 302-05.

Kayser, A. "Die Testamente der XII Patriarchen." *Beiträge zu den theologischen Wissenschaften in Verbindung mit der theologischen Gesellschaft zu Strassburg* 3 (1851): 107-40.

Langen, Joseph. *Das Judenthum in Palästina zur Zeit Christi. Ein Beitrag zur Offenbarungs- und Religions-Geschichte als Einleitung in die Theologie des Neuen Testaments.* Freiburg: Herder'sche Verlagshandlung, 1866.

Lardner, Nathaniel. *The Credibility of the Gospel History. Part II, or, the Principal Facts of the New Testament Confirmed by Passages of Ancient Authors, Who Were Contemporary with Our Savior or His Apostles, or Lived near Their Time.* London: [n.n.], 1735.

Lightfoot, J. B. *Saint Paul's Epistle to the Galatians; a Revised Text with Introduction, Notes, and Dissertations.* Reprint of 10th ed. London: Macmillan and Co., 1896.

Lücke, Friedrich. *Versuch einer vollständigen Einleitung in die Offenbarung Johannes.* 2nd ed. Bonn: Eduard Weber, 1852.

Migne, J.-P., ed. *Patrologiae cursus completus. Series graeca.* Paris: Paul Dupont, 1886.

Nitzsch, Carolus Immanuel. *De Testamentis duodecim Patriarchorum libro V.T. Pseudepigrapho.* Wittenberg: ex officina typographica Friderici Immanuelis Siebt., 1810.

Nitzsch, Friedrich. *Grundriss der christlichen Dogmengeschichte.* Berlin: Mittler und Sohn, 1870.

Paris, Matthew. *Chronica Majora.* Edited by Henry Richards Luard. 6 vols. London: Longman and Co., 1877.

Pick, B. "The Testaments of the Twelve Patriarchs." *Lutheran Church Review* 4 (1885): 161-86.

Renan, Ernest. *Histoire des origines du christianisme. L'église chrétienne.* Paris: Michel Lévy Fréres, 1879.

Reuss, E. *Die Geschichte der heiligen Schriften Neuen Testaments.* 5th ed. Braunschweig: C. A. Schwetschke und Sohn, 1874.

Ritschl, Albrecht. *Die Entstehung der altkatholischen Kirche. Eine kirchen- und dogmengeschichtliche Monographie.* Bonn: Adolph Marcus, 1850; 2nd ed. 1857.

Roberts, Alexander and Donaldson, James, eds. *The Ante-Nicene Fathers: Translations of the Writings of the Fathers down to A.D. 325.* 8 vols. Grand Rapids: Wm. B. Eerdmans Publishing Company, 1951.

Rönsch, H. *Das Buch der Jubiläen oder die kleine Genesis.* Leipzig: [n.n.], 1874.

Sinker, Robert. *Testamenta XII Patriarcharum: Appendix Containing a Collation of the Roman and Patmos mss. and Bibliographical Notes.* Cambridge: Deighton, Bell and Co., 1879.

_____. *The Testaments of the XII Patriarchs: An Attempt to Estimate Their Historic and Dogmatic Worth.* Cambridge: Deighton, Bell and Co., 1869.

Testament und Abschrifft der zwölf Patriarchen der Söhnen Jacobs. [n.p.]: Menradi Molteri und Augustini Lantzkroni, 1544.

Testamenta duodecim Patriarchu filiorum Jacob e greco in latinu versa: Roberto Linconiensi Episcopo interprete. [n.p.]: [n.n.].

Vorstman, Johannes Marinus. *Disquisitio de Testamentorum XII Patriarcharum.* Rotterdam: P. C. Hoog, 1857.

Warfield, B. B. "The Apologetical Value of the Testaments of the Twelve Patriarchs." *Presbyterian Review* 1 (1880): 58-84.

Wieseler, Carl. *Die 70 Wochen und die 63 Jahrwochen des Propheten Daniel erörtert und erläutert mit steter Rücksicht auf die biblischen Parallelen, auf Geschichte und Chronologie.* Göttingen: Vandenhoeck und Ruprecht, 1839.

B. Research from Schnapp through Charles

Baljon, J. M. S. "De Testamenten der XII Patriarchen." *Theologische Studiën-Utrecht* 4 (1886): 208-31.

Bousset, W. "Ein aramäisches Fragment des Testamentum Levi." *ZNW* 1 (1900): 344-46.

_____. "Die Testamente der XII Patriarchen: I. Die Ausscheidung der christlichen Interpolationen." *ZNW* 1 (1900): 141-75.

_____. "Die Testamente der XII Patriarchen: II. Composition und Zeit der judischen Grundschrift." *ZNW* 1 (1900): 187-209.

Budde, Karl, ed. *Geschichte der althebräischen Litteratur.* Leipzig: C. F. Amelangs, 1906.

Charles, R. H., ed. *The Apocrypha and Pseudepigrapha of the Old Testament in English with Introductions and Critical and Explanatory Notes to the Several Books.* 2 vols. Oxford: Clarendon, 1913.

_____, ed. *The Greek Versions of the Testaments of the Twelve Patriarchs, Edited from Nine MSS. together with the Variants of the Armenian and Slavonic Versions and Some Hebrew Fragments.* Oxford: Clarendon, 1908.

_____. "Man's Forgiveness of His Neighbor: A Study in Religious Development." *The Expositor*, 7th ser. 6 (1908): 492-505.

_____. "The Testaments of the XII. Patriarchs." *Encyclopedia Biblica* 1 (1899): 237-41.

_____. "Testaments of the XII Patriarchs." *A Dictionary of the Bible Dealing with Its Language, Literature and Contents* 4 (1909): 721-25.

_____. "The Testaments of the XII Patriarchs." *Hibbert Journal* 3 (1904-1905): 558-73.

_____, ed. *The Testaments of the Twelve Patriarchs, Translated from the Editor's Greek Text and Edited with Introduction, Notes, and Indices.* London: Adam and Charles Black, 1908.

_____ and Cowley, A. "An Early Source of the Testaments of the Twelve Patriarchs." *JQR* 19 (1907): 566-83.

Conybeare, F. C. "A Collation of Armenian Texts of the Testaments of (1) Judah; (2) Dan; (3) Joseph; (4) Benjamin." *JQR* 8 (1896): 471-85.

_____. "A Collation of Sinker's Texts of the Testaments of Reuben and Simeon with the Old Armenian Version." *JQR* 8 (1896): 260-68.

_____. "On the Jewish Authorship of the Testaments of the Twelve Patriarchs." *JQR* 5 (1893): 375-98.

_____. "The Testament of Job and the Testaments of the XII Patriarchs." *JQR* 13 (1900); 111-27 and 258-74.

Deane, William J. *Pseudepigrapha: An Account of Certain Apocryphal Sacred Writings of the Jews and Early Christians.* Edinburgh: T. and T. Clark, 1891.

Faye, Eugène de. *Les apocalypses juives: essai de critique littéraire et théologique.* Paris: Georges Bridel, 1892.

Gaster, M. "The Hebrew Text of One of the Testaments of the Twelve Patriarchs." *Society of Biblical Archeology: Proceedings* 16-17 (1894): 33-49.

Harnack, Adolf. *Geschichte der altchristlichen Litteratur bis Eusebius.* 2 vols. Leipzig: J. C. Hinrichs'sche Buchhandlung, 1897.

Issaverdens, J. *The Uncanonical Writings of the Old Testament Found in the Armenian MSS. of the Library of St. Lazarus, Venice.* Venice: Armenian Monastery, 1900.

Kautzsch, E., ed. *Die Apokryphen und Pseudepigraphen des Alten Testaments.* 2 vols. Tübingen: J. C. B. Mohr, 1900.

Kohler, K. "The Pre-Talmudic Haggada." *JQR* 5 (1893): 399-419.

_____. "Testaments of the Twelve Patriarchs." *The Jewish Encyclopedia* 12 (1906): 113-18.

Lawlor, H. J. "Early Citations from the Book of Enoch." *Journal of Philology* 25 (1897): 164-225.

Lévi, Israel. "Notes sur le texte araméen du Testament de Lévi récemment découvert." *Revue des études juives* 54 (1907): 166-80; 55 (1908): 285-87.

Marshall, J. "The Hebrew Text of One of the Testaments of the Twelve Patriarchs." *Society of Biblical Archeology: Proceedings* 16-17 (1894): 83-86.

Pass, H. Leonard and Arendzen, J. "Fragment of an Aramaic Text of the Testament of Levi." *JQR* 12 (1900): 651-61.

Preuschen, Erwin. "Die armenische Übersetzung der Testamente der zwölf Patriarchen." *ZNW* 1 (1900): 106-40.

Resch, G. "Das hebräische Testamentum Naphthali." *Theologische Studien und Kritiken* 72 (1899): 206-36.

Schlatter, A. *Israels Geschichte von Alexander dem Grossen bis Hadrian.* Stuttgart: Vereinsbuchhandlung, 1901.

_____. *Die Geschichte Israels von Alexander dem Grossen bis Hadrian.* 2nd ed. Stuttgart: Vereinsbuchhandlung, 1906.

Schnapp, Friedrich. *Die Testamente der zwölf Patriarchen untersucht.* Halle: Max Niemeyer, 1884.

Schürer, Emil. *Geschichte des jüdischen Volkes im Zeitalter Jesu Christi.* 3 vols. Leipzig: J. C. Hinrichs'sche Buchhandlung, 1886-1890.

_____. *A History of the Jewish People in the Time of Jesus Christ: First and Second Division.* Translated by John MacPherson, Sophie Taylor, and Peter Christie. 5 vols. New York: Scribner, 1891.

Volz, Paul. *Jüdische Eschatologie von Daniel bis Akiba.* Tübingen: J. C. B. Mohr, 1903.

C. Research from Charles through 1951

Aptowitzer, V. *Parteipolitik der Hasmonäerzeit im rabbinischen und pseudepigraphischen Schrifttum.* Vienna: Kohut Foundation, 1927.

Argyle, A. W. "The Influence of the Testaments of the Twelve Patriarchs upon the New Testament." *ExpT* 63 (1951-1952): 256-58.

Beasley-Murray, G. R. "The Two Messiahs in the Testaments of the Twelve Patriarchs." *JTS* 48 (1947): 1-12.

Bickerman, Elias J. "The Date of the Testaments of the Twelve Patriarchs." *JBL* 69 (1950): 245-60

Black, Matthew. "The Messiah in the Testament of Levi XVIII." *ExpT* 60 (1948-1949): 321-22.

Bonsirven, J. *Le judaïsme palestinien au temps de Jésus-Christ; sa théologie.* 2 vols. Paris: Gabriel Beauchesne et ses fils, 1934-1935.

Burkitt, F. Crawford. *Jewish and Christian Apocalypses.* London: H. Milford, 1914.

_____. Review of R. H. Charles, ed., *The Greek Versions of the Testaments of the Twelve Patriarchs. JTS* 10 (1908): 135-41.

Couchoud, P. L., ed. *Congrès d'histoire du christianisme.* 3 vols. Paris: Rieder, 1928.

Dibelius, Martin. *Der Hirt des Hermas.* Tübingen: J. C. B. Mohr, 1923.

Eppel, Robert. *Le piétisme juif dans les Testaments de douze patriarches.* Paris: Félix Alcan, 1930.

Fox, G. G. "Testaments of the Twelve Patriarchs." *The Universal Jewish Encyclopedia* 10 (1943): 202.

Ginzberg, Louis. "Eine unbekannte jüdische Sekte." *Monatsschrift für Geschichte und Wissenschaft des Judentums* 58 (1914): 395-429.

Herford, R. Travers. *Talmud and Apocrypha, a Comparative Study of the Jewish Ethical Teaching in the Rabbinical and Non-Rabbinical Sources in the Early Centuries.* London: Soncino, 1933.

Hunkin, J. W. "The Testaments of the Twelve Patriarchs." *JTS* 16 (1914): 80-97.

James, M. R. "The Venice Abstract from the Testaments of the Twelve Patriarchs." *JTS* 28 (1927): 337-48.

Karpeles, Gustav. *Geschichte der jüdischen Literatur.* 2 vols. 4th ed. Graz: Akademischer Druck, 1963.

Lagrange, M.-J. *Le judaïsme avant Jésus-Christ.* Paris: Librairie Lecoffre, 1931.

_____. *Le messianisme chez les juifs.* Paris: Victor Lecoffre, 1909.

Leszynsky, Rudolf. *Die Sadduzäer.* Berlin: Mayer und Müller, 1912.

Manson, T. W. "Testaments of the XII Patr.: Levi VIII." *JTS* 48 (1947): 59-61.

Mariès, L. "Le messie issu de Lévi chez Hippolyte de Rome." *RevScRel* 39 (1951): 381-96.

Messel, N. "Über die textkritisch begründete Ausscheidung vermutlicher christlicher Interpolationen in den Testamenten der zwölf Patriarchen." *BZAW* 33 (1918): 355-74.

Meyer, Ed. *Ursprung und Anfänge des Christentums.* 3 vols. Berlin: J. G. Cotta, 1921-1923.

Munch, P. A. "The Spirit in the Testaments of the Twelve Patriarchs." *AcOr* 13 (1935): 257-63.

Munck, Johannes. "Discours d'adieu dans le Nouveau Testament et dans la littérature biblique." In *Aux sources de la tradition chrétienne: Mélanges offerts à M. Maurice Goguel à l'occasion de son soixante-dixième anniversaire,* edited by Oscar Cullmann and Pierre Benoit, 155-70. Neuchâtel: Delachaux et Niestlé, 1950.

Perles, Felix. "Zur Erklärung der Testamente der zwölf Patriarchen." *Beihefte zur Orientalischen Litteraturzeitung* [2] (1908): 10-18.

Plummer, Alfred. "The Relations of the Testaments of the Twelve Patriarchs to the Books of the New Testament." *The Expositor,* 7th ser. 6 (1908): 481-91.

Porter, J. R. "The Messiah in the Testament of Levi XVIII." *ExpT* 61 (1949-1950): 90-91.

Riessler, Paul. *Altjüdisches Schrifttum ausserhalb der Bibel.* Augsburg: Dr. Benno Filfer Verlag, 1928.

Spitta, Friedrich. *Streitfragen der Geschichte Jesu.* Göttingen: Vandenhoeck und Ruprecht, 1907.

_____. *Zur Geschichte und Litteratur des Urchristentums.* 3 vols. Göttingen: Vandenhoeck und Ruprecht, 1893-1896.

Stauffer, E. "Abschiedsreden." *Reallexikon für Antike und Christentum* 1 (1950): 29-35.

_____. *Die Theologie des Neuen Testaments.* Genf: Oikumene Verlag, 1945.

Székely, Stephan. *Bibliotheca apocrypha: Introductio historico-critica in libros apocryphos utriusque Testamenti cum explicatione argumenti et doctrinae.* Freiburg: B. Herder, 1913.

Torrey, Charles Cutler. *The Apocryphal Literature, a Brief Introduction.* New Haven: Yale, 1945.

D. Research from 1952 to 1958

Aschermann, P. Hartmut. "Die paränetischen Formen der 'Testamente der zwölf Patriarchen' und ihr Nachwirken in der frühchristlichen Mahnung." Th.D. dissertation, Humboldt Universität-Berlin, 1955.

Audet, Jean-Paul. "Affinités littéraires et doctrinales du Manuel de discipline." *RB* 59 (1952): 219-38; 60 (1953): 41-82.

Bammel, Ernst. "Ἀρχιερεύς Προφητευῶν." *TLZ* 79 (1954): 351-56.

Brown, Raymond E. "The Messianism of Qumrân." *CBQ* 19 (1957): 53-82.

Burrows, Millar. *More Light on the Dead Sea Scrolls.* New York: Viking Press, 1958.

Chevallier, Max-Alain. *L'esprit et le messie dans le bas judaïsme et le Nouveau Testament.* Paris: Presses universitaires de France, 1958.

Cross, F. M. *The Ancient Library of Qumran and Modern Biblical Studies.* London: Gerald Duckworth, 1958.

Daniélou, Jean. *Les manuscrits de la mer Morte et les origines du christianisme.* Paris: Editions de l'Orante, 1957.

_____. Review of M. de Jonge, *The Testaments of the Twelve Patriarchs. RSR* 43 (1955): 564-67.

Delcor, M. "Dix ans de travaux sur les manuscrits de Qumrân." *Revue thomiste* 58 (1958): 734-79.

Doeve, J. W. Review of M. de Jonge, *The Testaments of the Twelve Patriarchs. Nederlands theologisch Tijdschrift* 9 (1954-1955): 49-52.

Dupont-Sommer, André. *Nouveaux aperçus sur des manuscrits de la mer Morte.* Paris: Maisonneuve, 1953.

Grant, Robert M. Review of M. de Jonge, *The Testaments of the Twelve Patriarchs. VC* 9 (1955): 185-86.

Grelot, Pierre. "Notes sur le testament araméen de Lévi: fragment de la Bodleian Library, Colonne a." *RB* 63 (1956): 391-406.

_____. "Le testament araméen de Lévi est-il traduit de l'hébreu?" *Revue des études juives* 14 (1955): 91-99.

Jeremias, Joachim. "Παῖς Θεοῦ im Spätjudentum in der Zeit nach der Entstehung der LXX." *TWNT* 5 (1954): 676-98.

Jones, D. R. Review of M. de Jonge, *The Testaments of the Twelve Patriarchs. Theology* 57 (1954): 390-92.

Jonge, M. de. *The Testaments of the Twelve Patriarchs: A Study of Their Text, Composition and Origin.* Assen: van Gorcum, 1953.

_____. "The Testaments of the Twelve Patriarchs and the New Testament." TU 73 (1959): 546-56.

Kuhn, Karl Georg. "Die beiden Messias Aarons und Israels." *NTS* 1 (1954-1955): 168-79.

_____. "Jesus in Gethsemane." *EvT* 12 (1952): 260-85.

Les manuscrits de la mer Morte: colloque de Strasbourg, 25-27 mai 1955. Paris: Presses universitaires de France, 1957.

Lods, Adolfe. *Histoire de la littérature hebraïque et juive depuis les origines jusq'à la ruine de l'état juif.* Paris: Payot, 1952.

Milik, J. T. "'Prière de Nabonide' et autres écrits d'un cycle de Daniel: fragments de Qumrân 4." *RB* 63 (1956): 407-15.

_____. "Le Testament de Lévi en araméen: fragment de la grotte 4 de Qumrân." *RB* 62 (1955): 398-406.

_____. Review of M. de Jonge, *The Testaments of the Twelve Patriarchs. RB* 62 (1955): 297-98.

Otzen, Benedikt. "Die neugefundenen hebräischen Sektenschriften und die Testamente der zwölf Patriarchen." *ST* 7 (1953): 125-57.

Rabin C. "The 'Teacher of Righteousness' in the 'Testaments of the Twelve Patriarchs?'" *JJS* 3 (1952): 127-28.

_____. *The Zadokite Documents.* Oxford: Clarendon, 1954.

Schubert, Kurt. "Testamentum Juda 24 im Lichte der Texte von Chirbet Qumran." *Wiener Zeitschrift für die Kunde des Morgenlands* 53 (1957): 227-36.

Sparks, H. F. D. Review of M. de Jonge, *The Testaments of the Twelve Patriarchs*. *JTS*, n.s. 6 (1955): 287-90.

Stendahl, Krister, ed. *The Scrolls and the New Testament*. New York: Harper and Brothers, 1957.

Woude, A. S. van der. *Die messianischen Vorstellungen der Gemeinde von Qumrân*. Assen: van Gorcum, 1957.

E. *Research from 1958 to the Present*

Baltzer, Klaus. *Das Bundesformular*. 2nd ed. Neukirchen-Vluyn: Neukirchener Verlag, 1964.

Becker, Jürgen. *Untersuchungen zur Entstehungsgeschichte der Testamente der zwölf Patriarchen*. Leiden: E. J. Brill, 1970.

Bernini, G. Review of M. Philonenko, *Les interpolations chrétiennes des Testaments des Douze Patriarches et les manuscrits de Qoumrân*. *Greg* 43 (1962): 335-37.

Blinzler, J., Kuss, O., and Mussner, F., eds. *Neutestamentliche Aufsätze: Festschrift für Prof. Josef Schmid zum 70. Geburtstag*. Regensburg: F. Pustet, 1963.

Boismard, M.-E. Review of M. Philonenko, *Les interpolations chrétiennes des Testaments des Douze Patriarches et les manuscrits de Qoumrân*. *RB* 68 (1961): 419-23.

Braun, F.-M. *Jean le théologien: les grandes traditions d'Israël et l'accord des Écritures selon le Quatrième Évangile*. Paris: Librarie Lecoffre, 1964.

_____. "Les Testaments des XII Patriarches et le problème de leur origine." *RB* 67 (1960): 516-49.

Bruce, F. F., ed. *Promise and Fulfillment: Essays Presented to Professor S. H. Hooke in Celebration of His Ninetieth Birthday, 21st January, 1964, by Members of the Society for Old Testament Study and Others*. Edinburgh: T. and T. Clark, 1963.

Burchard, Christoph. "Das Lamm in der Waagschale." *ZNW* 57 (1966): 219-28.

_____. "Neues zur Überlieferung der Testamente der zwölf Patriarchen." *NTS* 12 (1965-1966): 245-58.

_____. Review of M. de Jonge, ed., *Testamenta XII Patriarcharum*. *RQ* 5 (1965): 281-84.

Daniélou, Jean. *The Theology of Jewish Christianity*. Translated by John A. Baker. Chicago: H. Regnery, 1964.

Delling, G. Review of M. Philonenko, *Les interpolations chrétiennes des Testaments des Douze Patriarches et les manuscrits de Qoumrân*. *OLZ* 57 (1962): 48-50.

Denis, A.-M. *Introduction aux pseudépigraphes grecs d'Ancien Testament*. Leiden: E. J. Brill, 1970.

Dupont-Sommer, A. *Les écrits esséniens découverts près de la mer Morte*. Paris: Payot, 1959.

_____. *The Essene Writings from Qumran*. Translated by G. Vermes. Oxford: Blackwell, 1961.

Eissfeldt, Otto. *Einleitung in das Alte Testament unter Einschluss der Apokryphen und Pseudepigraphen sowie der apokryphen- und pseudepigraphenartigen Qumran-Schriften*. 3rd ed. Tübingen: J. C. B. Mohr, 1964.

Eltester, Walther, ed. *Studien zu den Testamenten der zwölf Patriarchen*. Berlin: Töpelmann, 1969.

Geoltrain, P. Review of M. Philonenko, *Les interpolations chrétiennes des Testaments des Douze Patriarches et les manuscrits de Qoumrân*. *RHPR* 41 (1961): 224-26.

Gnilka, Joachim. "Der Hymnus des Zacharias." *BZ* 6 (1962): 215-38.

Grelot, Pierre. "Le messie dans les apocryphes de l'Ancien Testament. État de la question." *Recherches bibliques* 6 (1962): 19-50.

Haupt, Detlev. "Das Testament des Levi: Untersuchungen zu seiner Entstehung und Überlieferungsgeschichte." Th.D. dissertation, Halle-Wittenberg, 1969.

Higgins, A. J. B. "The Priestly Messiah." *NTS* 13 (1966-1967): 211-39.

Hultgård, Anders. *Croyances messianiques des Test. XII Patr.: critique textuelle et commentaire des passages messianiques*. Uppsala: Skriv Services AB, 1971.

Jeremias, Joachim. "Das Lamm, das aus der Jungfrau hervorging: Test. Jos. 19.8." *ZNW* 57 (1966): 216-19.

Jonge, Henk Jan de. "Die Textüberlieferung der Testamente der zwölf Patriarchen." *ZNW* 63 (1972): 27-44.

Jonge, M. de. "Christian Influence in the Testaments of the Twelve Patriarchs." *NovT* 4 (1960): 182-235.

_____. "Once More: Christian Influence in the Testaments of the Twelve Patriarchs." *NovT* 5 (1962): 311-19.

_____, ed. *Testamenta XII Patriarcharum Edited according to Cambridge University Library MS Ff I.24 fol. 203a-262b with Short Notes.* Leiden: E. J. Brill, 1964; 2nd ed. 1970.

Koch, Klaus. "Das Lamm, das Ägypten vernichtet." *ZNW* 57 (1966): 79-93.

Le Déaut, Roger. "Le titre de Summus Sacerdos donné a Melchisedech est-il d'origine juive?" *RSR* 50 (1962): 222-29.

Leloir, Louis. Review of M. Stone, *The Testament of Levi. RQ* 7 (1970): 441-49.

Liver, J. "The Doctrine of the Two Messiahs in Sectarian Literature in the Time of the Second Commonwealth." *HTR* 52 (1959): 149-85.

Macky, Peter Wallace. *The Importance of the Teaching on God, Evil and Eschatology for the Dating of the Testaments of the Twelve Patriarchs.* Ann Arbor, Mich.: University Microfilms, 1971. (Th.D. dissertation, Princeton Theological Seminary, 1969.)

McKenzie, John L., ed. *The Bible in Current Catholic Thought.* New York: Herder and Herder, 1962.

Michel, Hans-Joachim. *Die Abschiedsrede des Paulus an die Kirche: Apg 20, 17-38.* Munich: Kösel Verlag, 1973.

Philonenko, Marc. "Les interpolations chrétiennes des Testaments des Douze Patriarches et les manuscrits de Qoumrân." *RHPR* 38 (1958): 309-43; 39 (1959): 14-38.

_____. *Les interpolations chrétiennes des Testaments des Douze Patriarches et les manuscrits de Qoumrân.* Paris: Presses universitaires de France, 1960.

Rese, Martin. "Überprüfung einiger Thesen von Joachim Jeremias zum Thema des Gottesknechtes im Judentum." *ZTK* 60 (1963): 21-41.

Ringgren, H. *The Faith of Qumran.* Translated by E. T. Sander. Philadelphia: Fortress Press, 1963.

Rost, L. "Testamente der XII Patriarchen." *RGG*³ 6 (1962): 701-02.

Smith, M. "The Testaments of the Twelve Patriarchs." *Interpreter's Dictionary of the Bible* 4 (1962): 575-79.

Steck, Odil Hannes. *Israel und das gewaltsame Geschick der Propheten: Untersuchungen zur Überlieferung des deuteronimistischen Geschichtsbildes im Alten Testament, Spätjudentum und Urchristentum.* Neukirchen-Vluyn: Neukirchener Verlag, 1967.

Stewart, R. A. "The Sinless High Priest." *NTS* 14 (1967-1968): 126-35.

Stone, Michael E. *The Testament of Levi: A First Study of the Armenian MSS of the Testaments of the XII Patriarchs in the Convent of St. James, Jerusalem, with Text, Critical Apparatus, Notes and Translation.* Jerusalem: St. James Press, 1969.

Turdeanu, Émile. "Les Testaments des douze patriarches en slave." *JSJ* 1 (1970): 148-84.

Wernberg-Møller, P. Review of M. Philonenko, *Les interpolations chrétiennes des Testaments des Douze Patriarches et les manuscrits de Qoumrân. JSS* 6 (1961): 292-93.